로마서·히브리서 쓰기를 시작하며 ✏️

로마서 • 히브리서 쓰기를 시작한 이유와 쓰고 난 후 기대하는 점 등을 기록해 보세요.

시작한 날

년.   월.   일.

십대를 위한
로마서·히브리서
영어로 한 달 쓰기
ESV®

일러두기

성경 본문은 Crossway가 발행한 The Holy Bible Standard Version(ESV)를 사용했습니다.

하루 한 장, 지혜가 트이고 공부습관이 잡힌다

십대를 위한 로마서·히브리서 영어로 한 달 쓰기 ESV®

사랑플러스 편집부 엮음

✚ 사랑플러스

성경 쓰기,
하나님의 지혜와 통하는 길

'나는 앞으로 무엇을 하면서 살아야 할까?'
'공부가 너무 힘들어. 어떻게 하면 잘할 수 있을까?'
'친구들이 나를 싫어하면 어쩌지?'
'부모님이 나 때문에 실망하시지는 않을까?'

답답하고 불안한 마음을 달래기 위해 스마트폰으로 친구들과 수다를 떨기도 하고, 코노(코인 노래방)에서 목청껏 노래도 해 보고, 게임에 빠져들기도 하지만 좀처럼 마음을 다잡을 수 없습니다.

우리는 이렇게 고민되는 순간을 수없이 마주하며 살아갑니다. 매번 어려운 선택의 기로에 놓이기도 하지요. 그때마다 우리는 무엇이 옳은 선택인지, 내가 과연 잘하고 있는 것인지 헷갈리기만 합니다. 누군가 '이럴 땐 이렇게 하고, 저럴 땐 저렇게 해야 한다'는 명확한 기준을 제시해 주면 좋겠다는 생각이 듭니다.

그렇다면 우리는 어떻게 중요한 일을 결정하고, 바른 선택을 할 수 있을까요? 해답은 바로 '지혜'에 있어요. 지혜는 바른 판단력과 분별력을 제공해 주는 보물과 같습니다. 지혜로운 사람이 되면 하나님이 원하시는 것이 무엇인지, 나를 향한 계획은 무엇인지 찾을 수 있어요. 하지만 지혜가 없으면 자기도 모르게 죄에 빠질 수 있고, 심지어 하나님을 떠나기도 해요.

그렇다면 지혜는 어떻게 얻을 수 있을까요? 하나님의 말씀인 성경이 바로 지혜가 가득 담긴 보물 창고입니다. 성경을 읽고 묵상하다 보면 '어떻게 사는 것이 잘 사는 인생'인지 명확하게 알 수 있지요.

읽기만 하면 될걸 귀찮고 시간도 없는데 왜 굳이 손으로 써야 할까요? 성경을 한 글자, 한 글자 천천히 따라 쓰다 보면 생각하는 시간이 생기기 때문에 말씀이 손과 머리 그리고 가슴 깊숙한 곳까지 뻗어 내려오는 걸 느낄 수 있어요. 중요한 말씀이 눈으로 슥 지나가지 않고 개념 하나하나가 생생하게 와닿는 경험을 할 수 있을 거예요. 뿐만 아니라 글을 잘 쓸 수 있는 능력이 생겨요. 좋은 문장을 따라 쓰면서 나도 모르는 사이에 어휘력과 문장력이 향상된답니다.

자, 이제 무궁무진한 지혜의 바다로 항해를 시작해 볼까요?

로마서와 히브리서

로마서는 복음의 정수를 보여 주는 책입니다. 구원은 예수 그리스도 한 분에 의해서만 이루어지며, 율법이 아닌 믿음으로 얻는다는 것을 분명하게 선포합니다. 로마서에는 복음과 교회에 대한 바울의 열정 및 그 열정을 풀어내는 날카로운 지성이 녹아 들어 있습니다.

히브리서는 기독교 신앙에서 떠나 유대교로 돌아가려는 유대인 그리스도인들을 격려하기 위해 쓴 책입니다. 예수 그리스도가 죄 없는 자신의 몸을 단 한 번의 제물로 바쳐 영원한 제사를 드리심으로 하나님과 인간을 화목하게 하신 대제사장임을 소개합니다.

로마서와 히브리서를 따라 쓰다 보면 복음을 분명하게 깨닫고 예수 그리스도만이 우리의 구원자이심을 확신하게 될 것입니다.

Romans 1

Greeting

1 Paul, a servant of Christ Jesus, called to be an apostle*, set apart for the gospel of God,

2 which he promised beforehand through his prophets in the holy Scriptures,

3 concerning his Son, who was descended from David according to the flesh

4 and was declared to be the Son of God in power according to the Spirit of holiness by his resurrection** from the dead, Jesus Christ our Lord,

5 through whom we have received grace and apostleship to bring about the obedience of faith for the sake of his name among all the nations,

6 including you who are called to belong to Jesus Christ,

7 To all those in Rome who are loved by God and called to be saints: Grace to you and peace from God our Father and the Lord Jesus Christ.

---

* apostle [ǝ́pɑːsl] ⑲ 사도. 주창자.

** resurrection [rèzǝrékʃǝn] ⑲ 부활. 재생.

Longing to Go to Rome

8   First, I thank my God through Jesus Christ for all of you,
    because your faith is proclaimed in all the world.

9   For God is my witness, whom I serve with my spirit in the gospel
    of his Son, that without ceasing* I mention you

10 always in my prayers, asking that somehow by God's will I may
    now at last succeed in coming to you.

11 For I long to see you, that I may impart to you some spiritual gift
    to strengthen you—

12 that is, that we may be mutually encouraged by each other's faith,
    both yours and mine.

13 I do not want you to be unaware, brothers, that I have often
    intended to come to you (but thus far have been prevented),
    in order that I may reap some harvest among you as well as among
    the rest of the Gentiles.

14 I am under obligation both to Greeks and to barbarians,
    both to the wise and to the foolish.

15 So I am eager to preach the gospel to you also who are in Rome.

The Righteous Shall Live by Faith

16 For I am not ashamed of the gospel, for it is the power of God for
    salvation to everyone who believes, to the Jew first and also to
    the Greek.

17 For in it the righteousness of God is revealed from faith for faith,
    as it is written, "The righteous shall live by faith."

---

*   ceasing [síːsiŋ] 옝 중지. 중단.

God's Wrath on Unrighteousness

18 For the wrath of God is revealed from heaven against all ungodliness and unrighteousness of men, who by their unrighteousness suppress the truth.

19 For what can be known about God is plain to them, because God has shown it to them.

20 For his invisible attributes, namely, his eternal power and divine* nature, have been clearly perceived, ever since the creation of the world, in the things that have been made. So they are without excuse.

21 For although they knew God, they did not honor him as God or give thanks to him, but they became futile** in their thinking, and their foolish hearts were darkened.

22 Claiming to be wise, they became fools,

23 and exchanged the glory of the immortal God for images resembling mortal man and birds and animals and creeping things.

24 Therefore God gave them up in the lusts of their hearts to impurity, to the dishonoring of their bodies among themselves,

25 because they exchanged the truth about God for a lie and worshiped and served the creature rather than the Creator, who is blessed forever! Amen.

26 For this reason God gave them up to dishonorable passions. For their women exchanged natural relations for those that are contrary to nature;

---

*   divine [diváin] ⑧ 신(神)의, 신성한, 종교적인 ⑨ 성직자 ⑤ 예언하다.
** futile [fjú:tl] ⑧ 헛된, 쓸데없는, 시시한.

27 and the men likewise gave up natural relations with women and were consumed with passion for one another, men committing shameless acts with men and receiving in themselves the due penalty for their error.

28 And since they did not see fit to acknowledge God, God gave them up to a debased mind to do what ought not to be done.

29 They were filled with all manner of unrighteousness, evil, covetousness*, malice**. They are full of envy, murder, strife, deceit, maliciousness. They are gossips,

30 slanderers, haters of God, insolent, haughty, boastful, inventors of evil, disobedient to parents,

31 foolish, faithless, heartless, ruthless.

32 Though they know God's righteous decree*** that those who practice such things deserve to die, they not only do them but give approval to those who practice them.

---

*   covetousness [kʌvitəsnis] 몡 탐욕, 탐냄, 갈망함.
**   malice [mǽlis] 몡 악의, 적의, 원한.
***   decree [dikríː] 몡 법령, 명령, 포고.

암송 구절 해설

For in it the righteousness of God is revealed from faith for faith,
as it is written, "The righteous shall live by faith." (1:17)

복음에는 하나님의 의가 나타나서 믿음으로 믿음에 이르게 하나니
기록된 바 오직 의인은 믿음으로 말미암아 살리라 함과 같으니라.

1장 16-17절은 로마서 전체의 주제를 담은 구절이라고 할 수 있습니다. 복음에는 구원의 능력이 있습니다. 복음에 하나님의 의가 나타나기 때문입니다. '하나님의 의'에는 하나님이 하시는 모든 선한 일과 공정한 심판 그리고 우리를 향한 사랑이 담겨 있습니다. 이러한 하나님의 의는 오직 믿음으로만 경험할 수 있습니다.

오늘 본문을 쓰면서 깨달은 지혜, 새롭게 다짐한 점,
떠오른 생각 등을 자유롭게 적어 보세요.

Romans 2

God's Righteous Judgment

1 Therefore you have no excuse, O man, every one of you who judges. For in passing judgment on another you condemn* yourself, because you, the judge, practice the very same things.

2 We know that the judgment of God rightly falls on those who practice such things.

3 Do you suppose, O man—you who judge those who practice such things and yet do them yourself—that you will escape the judgment of God?

4 Or do you presume on the riches of his kindness and forbearance and patience, not knowing that God's kindness is meant to lead you to repentance?

5 But because of your hard and impenitent heart you are storing up wrath for yourself on the day of wrath when God's righteous judgment will be revealed.

6 He will render to each one according to his works:

7 to those who by patience in well-doing seek for glory and honor and immortality, he will give eternal life;

---

* condemn [kəndém] ⑧ 비난하다, 선고를 내리다.

8 but for those who are self-seeking and do not obey the truth,
   but obey unrighteousness, there will be wrath and fury.

9 There will be tribulation* and distress for every human being who
   does evil, the Jew first and also the Greek,

10 but glory and honor and peace for everyone who does good,
   the Jew first and also the Greek.

11 For God shows no partiality.

God's Judgment and the Law

12 For all who have sinned without the law will also perish without
   the law, and all who have sinned under the law will be judged by
   the law.

13 For it is not the hearers of the law who are righteous before God,
   but the doers of the law who will be justified.

14 For when Gentiles, who do not have the law, by nature do what
   the law requires, they are a law to themselves, even though they do
   not have the law.

15 They show that the work of the law is written on their hearts,
   while their conscience also bears witness, and their conflicting
   thoughts accuse or even excuse them

16 on that day when, according to my gospel, God judges the secrets
   of men by Christ Jesus.

17 But if you call yourself a Jew and rely on the law and boast in God

18 and know his will and approve what is excellent, because you are
   instructed from the law;

---

*   tribulation [trìbjuléiʃən] ⑬ 시련, 고난, 재난.

19 and if you are sure that you yourself are a guide to the blind,
a light to those who are in darkness,

20 an instructor of the foolish, a teacher of children, having in
the law the embodiment* of knowledge and truth—

21 you then who teach others, do you not teach yourself?
While you preach against stealing, do you steal?

22 You who say that one must not commit adultery, do you commit
adultery? You who abhor idols, do you rob temples?

23 You who boast in the law dishonor God by breaking the law.

24 For, as it is written, "The name of God is blasphemed among
the Gentiles because of you."

25 For circumcision indeed is of value if you obey the law, but if you
break the law, your circumcision becomes uncircumcision.

26 So, if a man who is uncircumcised keeps the precepts of the law,
will not his uncircumcision be regarded as circumcision?

27 Then he who is physically uncircumcised but keeps the law will
condemn you who have the written code and circumcision but
break the law.

28 For no one is a Jew who is merely one outwardly,
nor is circumcision outward and physical.

29 But a Jew is one inwardly**, and circumcision is a matter of
the heart, by the Spirit, not by the letter. His praise is not from
man but from God.

---

* embodiment [imbάdimənt] ⑲ 구체화, 형상화, 모본.
** inwardly [ínwərdli] ⑲ 내부에서, 마음 깊이.

암송 구절 해설

For all who have sinned without the law will also perish without the law, and all who have sinned under the law will be judged by the law. (2:12)

무릇 율법 없이 범죄한 자는 또한 율법 없이 망하고
무릇 율법이 있고 범죄한 자는 율법으로 말미암아 심판을 받으리라.

하나님께서는 이스라엘 백성에게 율법을 주셨습니다. 그러나 단지 율법을 가졌다는 것만으로 구원이 보장되는 것은 아닙니다. 율법은 순종할 때만 유익이 있습니다. 그런데 하나님께 의롭다고 인정받을 만큼 율법에 순종할 수 있는 사람은 없기 때문에 그 누구도 율법을 통해서는 구원을 받을 수 없습니다. 구원은 오직 예수 그리스도를 믿는 믿음을 통해 은혜로만 가능합니다.

✎ 하루 한 문장, 생각 쓰기

오늘 본문을 쓰면서 깨달은 지혜, 새롭게 다짐한 점,
떠오른 생각 등을 자유롭게 적어 보세요.

Romans 3

God's Righteousness Upheld

1 Then what advantage has the Jew? Or what is the value of circumcision?

2 Much in every way. To begin with, the Jews were entrusted with the oracles of God.

3 What if some were unfaithful? Does their faithlessness nullify* the faithfulness of God?

4 By no means! Let God be true though every one were a liar, as it is written, "That you may be justified in your words, and prevail when you are judged."

5 But if our unrighteousness serves to show the righteousness of God, what shall we say? That God is unrighteous to inflict wrath on us? (I speak in a human way.)

6 By no means! For then how could God judge the world?

7 But if through my lie God's truth abounds to his glory, why am I still being condemned as a sinner?

8 And why not do evil that good may come?—as some people slanderously charge us with saying. Their condemnation is just.

---

* nullify [nʌləfài] ⑧ 무효로 하다. 파기하다.

No One Is Righteous

9 What then? Are we Jews any better off? No, not at all. For we have already charged that all, both Jews and Greeks, are under sin,

10 as it is written: "None is righteous, no, not one;

11 no one understands; no one seeks for God.

12 All have turned aside; together they have become worthless; no one does good, not even one."

13 "Their throat is an open grave; they use their tongues to deceive." "The venom* of asps is under their lips."

14 Their mouth is full of curses and bitterness."

15 "Their feet are swift to shed blood;

16 in their paths are ruin and misery,

17 and the way of peace they have not known."

18 "There is no fear of God before their eyes."

19 Now we know that whatever the law says it speaks to those who are under the law, so that every mouth may be stopped, and the whole world may be held accountable to God.

20 For by works of the law no human being will be justified in his sight, since through the law comes knowledge of sin.

The Righteousness of God Through Faith

21 But now the righteousness of God has been manifested apart from the law, although the Law and the Prophets bear witness to it—

22 the righteousness of God through faith in Jesus Christ for all who believe. For there is no distinction:

---

* venom [vénəm] ⑲ 독, 악의, ⑤ 독을 타다, 원한을 품다.

23 for all have sinned and fall short of the glory of God,

24 and are justified by his grace as a gift, through the redemption*
that is in Christ Jesus,

25 whom God put forward as a propitiation** by his blood,
to be received by faith. This was to show God's righteousness,
because in his divine forbearance he had passed over former sins.

26 It was to show his righteousness at the present time, so that he
might be just and the justifier of the one who has faith in Jesus.

27 Then what becomes of our boasting? It is excluded. By what kind
of law? By a law of works? No, but by the law of faith.

28 For we hold that one is justified by faith apart from works of
the law.

29 Or is God the God of Jews only? Is he not the God of Gentiles
also? Yes, of Gentiles also,

30 since God is one—who will justify the circumcised by faith and
the uncircumcised through faith.

31 Do we then overthrow the law by this faith? By no means!
On the contrary, we uphold the law.

---

*   redemption [ridémpʃən] ⑲ 속량, 되찾기, 구출, 속죄, 구원.

**   propitiation [prəpìʃiéiʃən] ⑲ 위로, 속죄.

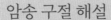

암송 구절 해설

And are justified by his grace as a gift,
through the redemption that is in Christ Jesus. (3:24)

그리스도 예수 안에 있는 속량으로 말미암아
하나님의 은혜로 값없이 의롭다 하심을 얻은 자 되었느니라.

'의롭다 하심'을 얻었다는 것은 하나님께서 죄가 없다고 선언하셨다는 뜻입니다. 하나님께서 그렇게 하신 이유는 우리가 그리스도 안에서 속량된 사람들이기 때문입니다. '속량'이란 노예 상태에 있던 누군가의 몸값을 지불하여 그를 자유롭게 풀어 주는 것입니다. 예수님은 자기의 생명을 몸값으로 지불하시고 우리에게 자유를 주셨습니다.

오늘 본문을 쓰면서 깨달은 지혜, 새롭게 다짐한 점,
떠오른 생각 등을 자유롭게 적어 보세요.

Romans 4

Abraham Justified by Faith

1 What then shall we say was gained by Abraham, our forefather according to the flesh?

2 For if Abraham was justified by works, he has something to boast about, but not before God.

3 For what does the Scripture say? "Abraham believed God, and it was counted to him as righteousness."

4 Now to the one who works, his wages are not counted as a gift but as his due.

5 And to the one who does not work but believes in him who justifies the ungodly, his faith is counted as righteousness,

6 just as David also speaks of the blessing of the one to whom God counts righteousness apart from works:

7 "Blessed are those whose lawless deeds are forgiven, and whose sins are covered;

8 blessed is the man against whom the Lord will not count his sin."

9 Is this blessing then only for the circumcised, or also for the uncircumcised? For we say that faith was counted to Abraham as righteousness.

10 How then was it counted to him? Was it before or after he had been circumcised? It was not after, but before he was circumcised.

11 He received the sign of circumcision as a seal of the righteousness that he had by faith while he was still uncircumcised. The purpose was to make him the father of all who believe without being circumcised, so that righteousness would be counted to them as well,

12 and to make him the father of the circumcised who are not merely circumcised but who also walk in the footsteps of the faith that our father Abraham had before he was circumcised.

The Promise Realized Through Faith

13 For the promise to Abraham and his offspring that he would be heir of the world did not come through the law but through the righteousness of faith.

14 For if it is the adherents* of the law who are to be the heirs, faith is null and the promise is void.

15 For the law brings wrath, but where there is no law there is no transgression.

16 That is why it depends on faith, in order that the promise may rest on grace and be guaranteed to all his offspring—not only to the adherent of the law but also to the one who shares the faith of Abraham, who is the father of us all,

17 as it is written, "I have made you the father of many nations"—in the presence of the God in whom he believed, who gives life to the dead and calls into existence the things that do not exist.

* adherent [ædhíːərənt] 명 추종자, 지지자, 형 편드는, 붙어 있는.

18 In hope he believed against hope, that he should become
    the father of many nations, as he had been told, "So shall your
    offspring be."

19 He did not weaken in faith when he considered his own body,
    which was as good as dead (since he was about a hundred years
    old), or when he considered the barrenness of Sarah's womb.

20 No unbelief made him waver concerning the promise of God,
    but he grew strong in his faith as he gave glory to God,

21 fully convinced that God was able to do what he had promised.

22 That is why his faith was "counted to him as righteousness."

23 But the words "it was counted to him" were not written for his
    sake alone,

24 but for ours also. It will be counted to us who believe in him who
    raised from the dead Jesus our Lord,

25 who was delivered up for our trespasses and raised for our
    justification.

암송 구절 해설

Who(Jesus) was delivered up for our trespasses
and raised for our justification. (4:25)

예수는 우리가 범죄한 것 때문에 내줌이 되고
또한 우리를 의롭다 하시기 위하여 살아나셨느니라.

25절은 예수님이 하신 중요한 일 두 가지를 설명합니다. 하나는 우리의 죄 문제를 해결하기 위해 자기의 생명을 던지신 것입니다. 다른 하나는 우리를 의롭게 만들기 위해 죽음에서 부활하신 것입니다. 이를 통해 우리는 생명을 얻을 뿐만 아니라 예수님과 깊은 관계를 맺게 되었습니다.

오늘 본문을 쓰면서 깨달은 지혜, 새롭게 다짐한 점,
떠오른 생각 등을 자유롭게 적어 보세요.

Romans 5

Peace with God Through Faith

1 Therefore, since we have been justified by faith, we have peace with God through our Lord Jesus Christ.

2 Through him we have also obtained access by faith into this grace in which we stand, and we rejoice in hope of the glory of God.

3 Not only that, but we rejoice in our sufferings, knowing that suffering produces endurance,

4 and endurance produces character, and character produces hope,

5 and hope does not put us to shame, because God's love has been poured into our hearts through the Holy Spirit who has been given to us.

6 For while we were still weak, at the right time Christ died for the ungodly*.

7 For one will scarcely die for a righteous person—though perhaps for a good person one would dare even to die—

8 but God shows his love for us in that while we were still sinners, Christ died for us.

---

* ungodly [ʌngɔ́dli] ⑱ 믿지 않는, 죄가 많은.

9   Since, therefore, we have now been justified by his blood,
    much more shall we be saved by him from the wrath of God.

10 For if while we were enemies we were reconciled* to God by
    the death of his Son, much more, now that we are reconciled,
    shall we be saved by his life.

11 More than that, we also rejoice in God through our Lord Jesus
    Christ, through whom we have now received reconciliation.

Death in Adam, Life in Christ

12 Therefore, just as sin came into the world through one man,
    and death through sin, and so death spread to all men because all
    sinned—

13 for sin indeed was in the world before the law was given, but sin is
    not counted where there is no law.

14 Yet death reigned from Adam to Moses, even over those whose
    sinning was not like the transgression of Adam, who was a type of
    the one who was to come.

15 But the free gift is not like the trespass. For if many died through
    one man's trespass, much more have the grace of God and the free
    gift by the grace of that one man Jesus Christ abounded for many.

16 And the free gift is not like the result of that one man's sin.
    For the judgment following one trespass brought condemnation,
    but the free gift following many trespasses brought justification.

---

*   reconcile [rékənsàil] 통 화해시키다, 중재하다, 조화시키다.

17 For if, because of one man's trespass, death reigned through that
one man, much more will those who receive the abundance of
grace and the free gift of righteousness reign in life through
the one man Jesus Christ.

18 Therefore, as one trespass led to condemnation for all men, so one
act of righteousness leads to justification and life for all men.

19 For as by the one man's disobedience the many were made sinners,
so by the one man's obedience the many will be made righteous.

20 Now the law came in to increase the trespass, but where sin
increased, grace abounded all the more,

21 so that, as sin reigned in death, grace also might reign through
righteousness leading to eternal life through Jesus Christ our Lord.

암송 구절 해설

But God shows his love for us in that while we were still sinners,
Christ died for us. (5:8)

우리가 아직 죄인 되었을 때에 그리스도께서 우리를 위하여 죽으심으로
하나님께서 우리에 대한 자기의 사랑을 확증하셨느니라.

국가나 왕, 부모, 배우자, 자녀 등 사랑하고 존경하는 대상을 위해 과감히 자기 목숨을
버리는 사람은 종종 있습니다. 하지만 자기와 아무런 관련이 없는 사람, 심지어 죄인을
위해 대신 죽을 사람은 없습니다. 예수님이 죄인 된 우리를 위해 대신 죽으셨다는 사실
은 그분이 우리를 얼마나 사랑하시는지 증명해 줍니다. 그래서 우리는 소망을 가지고
살아갈 수 있습니다.

✏️ 하루 한 문장, 생각 쓰기   오늘 본문을 쓰면서 깨달은 지혜, 새롭게 다짐한 점,
                            떠오른 생각 등을 자유롭게 적어 보세요.

Romans 6

Dead to Sin, Alive to God

1 What shall we say then? Are we to continue in sin that grace may abound?

2 By no means! How can we who died to sin still live in it?

3 Do you not know that all of us who have been baptized into Christ Jesus were baptized into his death?

4 We were buried therefore with him by baptism into death, in order that, just as Christ was raised from the dead by the glory of the Father, we too might walk in newness of life.

5 For if we have been united with him in a death like his, we shall certainly be united with him in a resurrection like his.

6 We know that our old self was crucified with him in order that the body of sin might be brought to nothing, so that we would no longer be enslaved to sin.

7 For one who has died has been set free from sin.

8 Now if we have died with Christ, we believe that we will also live with him.

9 We know that Christ, being raised from the dead, will never die again; death no longer has dominion over him.

10 For the death he died he died to sin, once for all, but the life he lives he lives to God.

11 So you also must consider yourselves dead to sin and alive to God in Christ Jesus.

12 Let not sin therefore reign in your mortal body, to make you obey its passions.

13 Do not present your members to sin as instruments for unrighteousness, but present yourselves to God as those who have been brought from death to life, and your members to God as instruments for righteousness.

14 For sin will have no dominion over you, since you are not under law but under grace.

Slaves to Righteousness

15 What then? Are we to sin because we are not under law but under grace? By no means!

16 Do you not know that if you present yourselves to anyone as obedient slaves, you are slaves of the one whom you obey, either of sin, which leads to death, or of obedience, which leads to righteousness?

17 But thanks be to God, that you who were once slaves of sin have become obedient from the heart to the standard of teaching to which you were committed,

18 and, having been set free from sin, have become slaves of righteousness.

19 I am speaking in human terms, because of your natural limitations. For just as you once presented your members as slaves to impurity and to lawlessness leading to more lawlessness, so now present your members as slaves to righteousness leading to sanctification.

20 For when you were slaves of sin, you were free in regard to righteousness.

21 But what fruit were you getting at that time from the things of which you are now ashamed? For the end of those things is death.

22 But now that you have been set free from sin and have become slaves of God, the fruit you get leads to sanctification and its end, eternal life.

23 For the wages of sin is death, but the free gift of God is eternal life in Christ Jesus our Lord.

암송 구절 해설

Do not present your members to sin as instruments for unrighteousness, but present yourselves to God as those who have been brought from death to life, and your members to God as instruments for righteousness. (6:13)

또한 너희 지체를 불의의 무기로 죄에게 내주지 말고
오직 너희 자신을 죽은 자 가운데서 다시 살아난 자같이 하나님께 드리며
너희 지체를 의의 무기로 하나님께 드리라.

죄에게 내준다는 것은 죄의 노예가 되어 섬긴다는 뜻입니다. 우리는 그리스도 안에서 새로운 신분을 받았기 때문에 더 이상 죄의 지배를 받을 이유가 없습니다. 우리의 주권을 하나님께 맡기고 구원받은 자답게 살아가야 합니다.

오늘 본문을 쓰면서 깨달은 지혜, 새롭게 다짐한 점,
떠오른 생각 등을 자유롭게 적어 보세요.

Romans 7

Released from the Law

1 Or do you not know, brothers—for I am speaking to those who know the law—that the law is binding on* a person only as long as he lives?

2 For a married woman is bound by law to her husband while he lives, but if her husband dies she is released from the law of marriage.

3 Accordingly, she will be called an adulteress if she lives with another man while her husband is alive. But if her husband dies, she is free from that law, and if she marries another man she is not an adulteress.

4 Likewise, my brothers, you also have died to the law through the body of Christ, so that you may belong to another, to him who has been raised from the dead, in order that we may bear fruit for God.

5 For while we were living in the flesh, our sinful passions, aroused** by the law, were at work in our members to bear fruit for death.

---

*   be binding on ~가 준수할 의무가 있다.
**   arouse [əráuz] ⑧ 불러일으키다, 유발하다, 자극하다.

6 But now we are released from the law, having died to that which held us captive, so that we serve in the new way of the Spirit and not in the old way of the written code.

The Law and Sin

7 What then shall we say? That the law is sin? By no means! Yet if it had not been for the law, I would not have known sin. For I would not have known what it is to covet if the law had not said, "You shall not covet."

8 But sin, seizing an opportunity through the commandment*, produced in me all kinds of covetousness. For apart from the law, sin lies dead.

9 I was once alive apart from the law, but when the commandment came, sin came alive and I died.

10 The very commandment that promised life proved to be death to me.

11 For sin, seizing an opportunity through the commandment, deceived me and through it killed me.

12 So the law is holy, and the commandment is holy and righteous and good.

13 Did that which is good, then, bring death to me? By no means! It was sin, producing death in me through what is good, in order that sin might be shown to be sin, and through the commandment might become sinful beyond measure.

14 For we know that the law is spiritual, but I am of the flesh, sold under sin.

---

* commandment [kəmǽndmənt] 통 계명. 명령.

15 For I do not understand my own actions. For I do not do what I want, but I do the very thing I hate.

16 Now if I do what I do not want, I agree with the law, that it is good.

17 So now it is no longer I who do it, but sin that dwells* within me.

18 For I know that nothing good dwells in me, that is, in my flesh. For I have the desire to do what is right, but not the ability to carry it out.

19 For I do not do the good I want, but the evil I do not want is what I keep on doing.

20 Now if I do what I do not want, it is no longer I who do it, but sin that dwells within me.

21 So I find it to be a law that when I want to do right, evil lies close at hand.

22 For I delight in the law of God, in my inner being,

23 but I see in my members another law waging war against the law of my mind and making me captive to the law of sin that dwells in my members.

24 Wretched man that I am! Who will deliver me from this body of death?

25 Thanks be to God through Jesus Christ our Lord! So then, I myself serve the law of God with my mind, but with my flesh I serve the law of sin.

---

* dwell [dwel] ⑧ 살다, 존재하다, 머무르다.

암송 구절 해설

So I find it to be a law that when I want to do right,
evil lies close at hand. (7:21)

그러므로 내가 한 법을 깨달았노니
곧 선을 행하기 원하는 나에게 악이 함께 있는 것이로다.

여기에서 '법'은 '원리'를 뜻한다고 볼 수 있습니다. 바울은 자기에게 선한 일을 하려는
열망이 있으나 자기 안에 여전히 죄가 남아 있음을 발견합니다. 하나님의 뜻을 거스르
는 악한 성향이 뿌리를 깊이 박고 있기 때문입니다. 우리의 힘으로는 죄를 이길 수 없
습니다. 예수 그리스도만이 삶 속에서 끊임없이 일어나는 죄 문제의 해답입니다.

✎ 하루 한 문장, 생각 쓰기

오늘 본문을 쓰면서 깨달은 지혜, 새롭게 다짐한 점.
떠오른 생각 등을 자유롭게 적어 보세요.

Romans 8

Life in the Spirit

1   There is therefore now no condemnation for those who are in Christ Jesus.

2   <u>For the law of the Spirit of life has set you free in Christ Jesus from the law of sin and death.</u>

3   For God has done what the law, weakened by the flesh, could not do. By sending his own Son in the likeness of sinful flesh and for sin, he condemned sin in the flesh,

4   in order that the righteous requirement of the law might be fulfilled in us, who walk not according to the flesh but according to the Spirit.

5   For those who live according to the flesh set their minds on the things of the flesh, but those who live according to the Spirit set their minds on the things of the Spirit.

6   For to set the mind on the flesh is death, but to set the mind on the Spirit is life and peace.

7   For the mind that is set on the flesh is hostile* to God, for it does not submit to God's law; indeed, it cannot.

---

*   hostile [hάstl] ⑱ 적대적인, 적의를 가진.

8   Those who are in the flesh cannot please God.

9   You, however, are not in the flesh but in the Spirit, if in fact
the Spirit of God dwells in you. Anyone who does not have
the Spirit of Christ does not belong to him.

10 But if Christ is in you, although the body is dead because of sin,
the Spirit is life because of righteousness.

11 If the Spirit of him who raised Jesus from the dead dwells in you,
he who raised Christ Jesus from the dead will also give life to your
mortal bodies through his Spirit who dwells in you.

Heirs with Christ

12 So then, brothers, we are debtors, not to the flesh,
to live according to the flesh.

13 For if you live according to the flesh you will die, but if by
the Spirit you put to death the deeds of the body, you will live.

14 For all who are led by the Spirit of God are sons of God.

15 For you did not receive the spirit of slavery to fall back into fear,
but you have received the Spirit of adoption* as sons, by whom we
cry, "Abba! Father!"

16 The Spirit himself bears witness with our spirit that we are
children of God,

17 and if children, then heirs—heirs of God and fellow heirs with
Christ, provided we suffer with him in order that we may also be
glorified with him.

---

*   adoption [ədάpʃən] ⑲ 채택, 양자 입양.

Future Glory

18 For I consider that the sufferings of this present time are not worth comparing with the glory that is to be revealed to us.

19 For the creation waits with eager longing for the revealing of the sons of God.

20 For the creation was subjected to futility*, not willingly**, but because of him who subjected it, in hope

21 that the creation itself will be set free from its bondage to corruption and obtain the freedom of the glory of the children of God.

22 For we know that the whole creation has been groaning together in the pains of childbirth until now.

23 And not only the creation, but we ourselves, who have the firstfruits of the Spirit, groan*** inwardly as we wait eagerly for adoption as sons, the redemption of our bodies.

24 For in this hope we were saved. Now hope that is seen is not hope. For who hopes for what he sees?

25 But if we hope for what we do not see, we wait for it with patience.

26 Likewise the Spirit helps us in our weakness. For we do not know what to pray for as we ought, but the Spirit himself intercedes for us with groanings too deep for words.

---

*   futility [fju:tíləti] ⑲ 무익, 헛됨.
** willingly [wíliŋli] ⑨ 기꺼이, 자진해서.
*** groan [groun] ⑲ 신음, ⑤ 신음하다, 괴로워하다.

27 And he who searches hearts knows what is the mind of the Spirit, because the Spirit intercedes for the saints according to the will of God.

28 And we know that for those who love God all things work together for good, for those who are called according to his purpose.

29 For those whom he foreknew he also predestined to be conformed to the image of his Son, in order that he might be the firstborn among many brothers.

30 And those whom he predestined he also called, and those whom he called he also justified, and those whom he justified he also glorified.

God's Everlasting Love

31 What then shall we say to these things? If God is for us, who can be against us?

32 He who did not spare his own Son but gave him up for us all, how will he not also with him graciously give us all things?

33 Who shall bring any charge against God's elect? It is God who justifies.

34 Who is to condemn? Christ Jesus is the one who died—more than that, who was raised—who is at the right hand of God, who indeed is interceding for us.

35 Who shall separate us from the love of Christ? Shall tribulation, or distress, or persecution*, or famine, or nakedness, or danger, or sword?

---

* persecution [pə̀ːrsikjúːʃən] 명 박해, 학대, 처형.

36 As it is written, "For your sake we are being killed all the day long; we are regarded as sheep to be slaughtered."

37 No, in all these things we are more than conquerors* through him who loved us.

38 For I am sure that neither death nor** life, nor angels nor rulers, nor things present nor things to come, nor powers,

39 nor height nor depth, nor anything else in all creation, will be able to separate us from the love of God in Christ Jesus our Lord.

---

*   conqueror [kάŋkərər] ⑲ 승리자, 정복자.

**   neither A nor B A도 아니고 B도 아니다.

암송 구절 해설

For the law of the Spirit of life has set you free in Christ Jesus
from the law of sin and death. (8:2)
이는 그리스도 예수 안에 있는 생명의 성령의 법이
죄와 사망의 법에서 너를 해방하였음이라.

우리가 죄에서 벗어날 수 있었던 이유는 그리스도를 믿음으로 그분과 하나가 되었기 때문입니다. 하나님은 아들을 제물로 보내셔서 우리의 죄에 대한 대가를 지불하셨고, 그 결과로 성령은 죄와 사망의 권세에서 우리를 해방시키셨습니다.

오늘 본문을 쓰면서 깨달은 지혜, 새롭게 다짐한 점,
떠오른 생각 등을 자유롭게 적어 보세요.

Romans 9

God's Sovereign Choice

1   I am speaking the truth in Christ—I am not lying; my conscience bears me witness in the Holy Spirit—

2   that I have great sorrow and unceasing anguish* in my heart.

3   For I could wish that I myself were accursed and cut off from Christ for the sake of my brothers, my kinsmen according to the flesh.

4   They are Israelites, and to them belong the adoption, the glory, the covenants, the giving of the law, the worship, and the promises.

5   To them belong the patriarchs, and from their race, according to the flesh, is the Christ, who is God over all, blessed forever. Amen.

6   But it is not as though the word of God has failed. For not all who are descended from Israel belong to Israel,

7   and not all are children of Abraham because they are his offspring, but "Through Isaac shall your offspring be named."

---

*   anguish [ǽŋgwiʃ] ⑲ 고통, ⑧ 괴롭히다, 괴로워하다.

8   This means that it is not the children of the flesh who are
    the children of God, but the children of the promise are counted
    as offspring.

9   For this is what the promise said: "About this time next year I will
    return, and Sarah shall have a son."

10 And not only so, but also when Rebekah had conceived children
    by one man, our forefather Isaac,

11 though they were not yet born and had done nothing either good
    or bad—in order that God's purpose of election might continue,
    not because of works but because of him who calls—

12 she was told, "The older will serve the younger."

13 As it is written, "Jacob I loved, but Esau I hated."

14 What shall we say then? Is there injustice on God's part?
    By no means!

15 For he says to Moses, "I will have mercy on whom I have mercy,
    and I will have compassion on whom I have compassion."

16 So then it depends not on human will or exertion*, but on God,
    who has mercy.

17 For the Scripture says to Pharaoh, "For this very purpose I have
    raised you up, that I might show my power in you, and that my
    name might be proclaimed in all the earth."

18 So then he has mercy on whomever he wills, and he hardens
    whomever he wills.

19 You will say to me then, "Why does he still find fault? For who
    can resist his will?"

---

*   exertion [igzə́:rʃən] 몡 노력, (능력을) 행사.

20 But who are you, O man, to answer back to God? Will what is molded say to its molder, "Why have you made me like this?"

21 Has the potter* no right over the clay, to make out of the same lump** one vessel for honorable use and another for dishonorable use?

22 What if God, desiring to show his wrath and to make known his power, has endured with much patience vessels of wrath prepared for destruction,

23 in order to make known the riches of his glory for vessels of mercy, which he has prepared beforehand for glory—

24 even us whom he has called, not from the Jews only but also from the Gentiles?

25 As indeed he says in Hosea, "Those who were not my people I will call 'my people,' and her who was not beloved I will call 'beloved.'"

26 "And in the very place where it was said to them, 'You are not my people,' there they will be called 'sons of the living God.'"

27 And Isaiah cries out concerning Israel: "Though the number of the sons of Israel be as the sand of the sea, only a remnant of them will be saved,

28 for the Lord will carry out his sentence upon the earth fully and without delay."

29 And as Isaiah predicted, "If the Lord of hosts had not left us offspring, we would have been like Sodom and become like Gomorrah."

---

* potter [pɑ́tər] ⑲ 도공. 옹기장이.

** lump [lʌmp] ⑲ 덩어리. 혹. ⑧ 덩어리가 지다. 함께 묶다.

Israel's Unbelief

30 What shall we say, then? <u>That Gentiles who did not pursue righteousness have attained* it, that is, a righteousness that is by faith;</u>

31 but that Israel who pursued a law that would lead to righteousness did not succeed in reaching that law.

32 Why? Because they did not pursue it by faith, but as if it were based on works. They have stumbled over the stumbling stone,

33 as it is written, "Behold, I am laying in Zion** a stone of stumbling, and a rock of offense; and whoever believes in him will not be put to shame."

---

* attain [ətéin] ⑧ 달성하다, 도달하다.

** Zion [záiən] ⑲ 시온(예루살렘에 있는 언덕), 유대 민족, 하늘의 예루살렘.

암송 구절 해설

That Gentiles who did not pursue righteousness have attained it,
that is, a righteousness that is by faith. (9:30b)

의를 따르지 아니한 이방인들이 의를 얻었으니 곧 믿음에서 난 의요.

하나님의 의는 간절히 바라거나 노력한다고 해서 손에 넣을 수 있는 것이 아닙니다. 오직 긍휼히 여기시는 하나님의 은혜로 얻을 수 있습니다. 30절은 그 증거입니다. 예수님을 거부한 유대인들은 남은 자만 구원을 얻지만(27절), 복음을 받아들인 이방인들은 믿음으로 의롭게 되었습니다.

✏️ 하루 한 문장, 생각 쓰기   오늘 본문을 쓰면서 깨달은 지혜, 새롭게 다짐한 점,
떠오른 생각 등을 자유롭게 적어 보세요.

Romans 10

The Message of Salvation to All

1 Brothers, my heart's desire and prayer to God for them is that they may be saved.

2 For I bear them witness that they have a zeal for God, but not according to knowledge.

3 For, being ignorant of the righteousness of God, and seeking to establish their own, they did not submit to God's righteousness.

4 For Christ is the end of the law for righteousness to everyone who believes.

5 For Moses writes about the righteousness that is based on the law, that the person who does the commandments shall live by them.

6 But the righteousness based on faith says, "Do not say in your heart, 'Who will ascend* into heaven?'" (that is, to bring Christ down)

7 "or 'Who will descend into the abyss?'" (that is, to bring Christ up from the dead).

8 But what does it say? "The word is near you, in your mouth and in your heart" (that is, the word of faith that we proclaim);

---

* ascend [əsénd] ⑧ 오르다, 상승하다.

9   because, if you confess with your mouth that Jesus is Lord and believe in your heart that God raised him from the dead, you will be saved.

10 For with the heart one believes and is justified, and with the mouth one confesses and is saved.

11 For the Scripture says, "Everyone who believes in him will not be put to shame."

12 For there is no distinction between Jew and Greek; for the same Lord is Lord of all, bestowing* his riches on all who call on him.

13 For "everyone who calls on the name of the Lord will be saved."

14 How then will they call on him in whom they have not believed? And how are they to believe in him of whom they have never heard? And how are they to hear without someone preaching?

15 And how are they to preach unless they are sent? As it is written, "How beautiful are the feet of those who preach the good news!"

16 But they have not all obeyed the gospel. For Isaiah says, "Lord, who has believed what he has heard from us?"

17 So faith comes from hearing, and hearing through the word of Christ.

18 But I ask, have they not heard? Indeed they have, for "Their voice has gone out to all the earth, and their words to the ends of the world."

19 But I ask, did Israel not understand? First Moses says, "I will make you jealous of those who are not a nation; with a foolish nation I will make you angry."

---

*   bestow [bistóu] ⑧ 수여하다, 쓰다.

20 Then Isaiah is so bold as to say, "I have been found by those who did not seek me; I have shown myself to those who did not ask for me."

21 But of Israel he says, "All day long I have held out my hands to a disobedient and contrary people."

암송 구절 해설

For with the heart one believes and is justified,
and with the mouth one confesses and is saved. (10:10)
사람이 마음으로 믿어 의에 이르고 입으로 시인하여 구원에 이르느니라.

하나님은 이미 우리를 의롭게 하기 위한 준비를 마치셨습니다. 우리는 마음으로 믿고 입으로 고백하면 됩니다. 입으로 시인하는 것은 믿음의 증거입니다. 그리스도를 진정으로 믿는 사람들은 소리 내어 고백할 수밖에 없습니다.

✎ 하루 한 문장, 생각 쓰기   오늘 본문을 쓰면서 깨달은 지혜, 새롭게 다짐한 점,
떠오른 생각 등을 자유롭게 적어 보세요.

Romans 11

The Remnant of Israel

1   I ask, then, has God rejected his people? By no means! For I myself am an Israelite, a descendant of Abraham, a member of the tribe of Benjamin.

2   God has not rejected his people whom he foreknew*. Do you not know what the Scripture says of Elijah, how he appeals to God against Israel?

3   "Lord, they have killed your prophets, they have demolished your altars, and I alone am left, and they seek my life."

4   But what is God's reply to him? "I have kept for myself seven thousand men who have not bowed the knee to Baal."

5   So too at the present time there is a remnant, chosen by grace.

6   But if it is by grace, it is no longer on the basis of works; otherwise grace would no longer be grace.

7   What then? Israel failed to obtain what it was seeking. The elect obtained it, but the rest were hardened,

8   as it is written, "God gave them a spirit of stupor, eyes that would not see and ears that would not hear, down to this very day."

---

*   foreknow [fɔ́:rnóu] ⑧ 미리 알다, 예지하다.

9　And David says, "Let their table become a snare and a trap,
　　a stumbling block and a retribution for them;

10　let their eyes be darkened so that they cannot see, and bend their
　　backs forever."

Gentiles Grafted In

11　So I ask, did they stumble in order that they might fall?
　　By no means! Rather, through their trespass salvation has come to
　　the Gentiles, so as to make Israel jealous.

12　Now if their trespass means riches for the world, and if their
　　failure means riches for the Gentiles, how much more will their
　　full inclusion mean!

13　Now I am speaking to you Gentiles. Inasmuch then as I am
　　an apostle to the Gentiles, I magnify my ministry

14　in order somehow to make my fellow Jews jealous, and thus save
　　some of them.

15　For if their rejection means the reconciliation of the world,
　　what will their acceptance mean but life from the dead?

16　If the dough offered as firstfruits is holy, so is the whole lump,
　　and if the root is holy, so are the branches.

17　But if some of the branches were broken off, and you, although
　　a wild olive shoot, were grafted* in among the others and now
　　share in the nourishing root of the olive tree,

18　do not be arrogant toward the branches. If you are, remember it is
　　not you who support the root, but the root that supports you.

---

*　graft [græft] ⑲ 접붙임, 이식, 접목. ⑧ 접붙이다.

19 Then you will say, "Branches were broken off so that I might be grafted in."

20 That is true. They were broken off because of their unbelief, but you stand fast through faith. So do not become proud, but fear.

21 For if God did not spare the natural branches, neither will he spare you.

22 Note then the kindness and the severity* of God: severity toward those who have fallen, but God's kindness to you, provided you continue in his kindness. Otherwise you too will be cut off.

23 And even they, if they do not continue in their unbelief, will be grafted in, for God has the power to graft them in again.

24 For if you were cut from what is by nature a wild olive tree, and grafted, contrary to nature, into a cultivated olive tree, how much more will these, the natural branches, be grafted back into their own olive tree.

The Mystery of Israel's Salvation

25 Lest you be wise in your own sight, I do not want you to be unaware of this mystery, brothers: a partial hardening has come upon Israel, until the fullness of the Gentiles has come in.

26 And in this way all Israel will be saved, as it is written, "The Deliverer will come from Zion, he will banish ungodliness from Jacob";

27 "and this will be my covenant with them when I take away their sins."

---

* severity [səvérəti] ⑲ 엄격, 가혹, 준엄.

28 As regards the gospel, they are enemies for your sake. But as regards election, they are beloved for the sake of their forefathers.

29 For the gifts and the calling of God are irrevocable[*].

30 For just as you were at one time disobedient to God but now have received mercy because of their disobedience,

31 so they too have now been disobedient in order that by the mercy shown to you they also may now receive mercy.

32 <u>For God has consigned all to disobedience, that he may have mercy on all.</u>

33 Oh, the depth of the riches and wisdom and knowledge of God! How unsearchable are his judgments and how inscrutable[**] his ways!

34 "For who has known the mind of the Lord, or who has been his counselor?"

35 "Or who has given a gift to him that he might be repaid?"

36 For from him and through him and to him are all things. To him be glory forever. Amen.

---

[*]   irrevocable [irévəkəbl] ⑧ 돌이킬 수 없는, 폐지할 수 없는.

[**]   inscrutable [inskrú:təbl] ⑧ 헤아릴 수 없는, 불가사의한, 심오한.

암송 구절 해설

For God has consigned all to disobedience,
that he may have mercy on all. (11:32)

하나님이 모든 사람을 순종하지 아니하는 가운데 가두어 두심은
모든 사람에게 긍휼을 베풀려 하심이로다.

'모든 사람'은 유대인과 이방인 전부를 가리키는 말입니다. 이스라엘은 주님께 순종하지 않았지만 언젠가는 하나님께서 그들의 완고함을 없애 주실 것이며, 그때 하나님의 자비가 모든 사람에게 '차별 없이' 임할 것입니다.

오늘 본문을 쓰면서 깨달은 지혜, 새롭게 다짐한 점,
떠오른 생각 등을 자유롭게 적어 보세요.

Romans 12

A Living Sacrifice

1   I appeal to you therefore, brothers, by the mercies of God,
    to present your bodies as a living sacrifice, holy and acceptable to
    God, which is your spiritual worship.

2   Do not be conformed to this world, but be transformed by
    the renewal of your mind, that by testing you may discern* what is
    the will of God, what is good and acceptable and perfect.

Gifts of Grace

3   For by the grace given to me I say to everyone among you not to
    think of himself more highly than he ought to think, but to think
    with sober** judgment, each according to the measure of faith that
    God has assigned.

4   For as in one body we have many members, and the members do
    not all have the same function,

5   so we, though many, are one body in Christ, and individually
    members one of another.

---

*   discern [disə́:rn] ⑧ 분별하다, 식별하다, 인식하다.
**   sober [sóubər] ⑨ 냉정한, 침착한, 균형 있는.

6　Having gifts that differ according to the grace given to us, let us use them: if prophecy, in proportion to our faith;

7　if service, in our serving; the one who teaches, in his teaching;

8　the one who exhorts*, in his exhortation; the one who contributes, in generosity; the one who leads, with zeal; the one who does acts of mercy, with cheerfulness.

Marks of the True Christian

9　Let love be genuine. Abhor what is evil; hold fast to what is good.

10　Love one another with brotherly affection. Outdo one another in showing honor.

11　Do not be slothful in zeal, be fervent** in spirit, serve the Lord.

12　Rejoice in hope, be patient in tribulation, be constant in prayer.

13　Contribute to the needs of the saints and seek to show hospitality.

14　Bless those who persecute you; bless and do not curse them.

15　Rejoice with those who rejoice, weep with those who weep.

16　Live in harmony with one another. Do not be haughty, but associate with the lowly. Never be wise in your own sight.

17　Repay no one evil for evil, but give thought to do what is honorable in the sight of all.

18　If possible, so far as it depends on you, live peaceably with all.

19　Beloved, never avenge yourselves, but leave it to the wrath of God, for it is written, "Vengeance is mine, I will repay, says the Lord."

---

*　exhort [igzɔ́:rt] ⑧ 권하다. 권고하다. 훈계하다.

**　fervent [fə́:rvənt] (형) 열심을 내는, 열렬한, 뜨거운.

20 To the contrary, "if your enemy is hungry, feed him; if he is thirsty, give him something to drink; for by so doing you will heap* burning coals** on his head."

21 Do not be overcome by evil, but overcome evil with good.

---

*   heap [hiːp] ⑲ 더미. ⑧ 쌓다. 축적하다.
**   coal [koul] ⑲ 석탄. 숯.

암송 구절 해설

Do not be conformed to this world, but be transformed
by the renewal of your mind, that by testing you may discern
what is the will of God, what is good and acceptable and perfect. (12:2)

너희는 이 세대를 본받지 말고 오직 마음을 새롭게 함으로 변화를 받아
하나님의 선하시고 기뻐하시고 온전하신 뜻이 무엇인지 분별하도록 하라.

그리스도인으로 어떤 자세와 방식으로 세상을 살아가야 하는지 알려 주는 구절입니다. 우리의 마음은 세상을 닮지 말아야 하고 우리의 삶 자체가 하나님께 드리는 예배가 되어야 합니다. 우리 안에 있는 성령은 우리가 마음을 새롭게 하여 변화되도록 도와주시며, 그럴 때 우리가 마주하는 모든 상황에서 하나님의 뜻을 분별할 수 있습니다.

오늘 본문을 쓰면서 깨달은 지혜, 새롭게 다짐한 점,
떠오른 생각 등을 자유롭게 적어 보세요.

Romans 13

Submission to the Authorities

1   Let every person be subject to the governing authorities.
    For there is no authority except from God, and those that exist
    have been instituted by God.

2   Therefore whoever resists the authorities resists what God has
    appointed, and those who resist will incur* judgment.

3   For rulers are not a terror to good conduct, but to bad. Would you
    have no fear of the one who is in authority? Then do what is good,
    and you will receive his approval,

4   for he is God's servant for your good. But if you do wrong,
    be afraid, for he does not bear the sword in vain. For he is
    the servant of God, an avenger who carries out God's wrath on
    the wrongdoer**.

5   Therefore one must be in subjection, not only to avoid God's
    wrath but also for the sake of conscience.

6   For because of this you also pay taxes, for the authorities are
    ministers of God, attending to this very thing.

---

*   incur [inkə́:r] ⑧ 초래하다, 발생시키다.

**   wrongdoer [rɔ́:ŋduːər] ⑱ 범죄자, 죄인.

7　Pay to all what is owed to them: taxes to whom taxes are owed, revenue to whom revenue is owed, respect to whom respect is owed, honor to whom honor is owed.

Fulfilling the Law Through Love

8　<u>Owe no one anything, except to love each other, for the one who loves another has fulfilled the law.</u>

9　For the commandments, "You shall not commit adultery, You shall not murder, You shall not steal, You shall not covet," and any other commandment, are summed up in this word: "You shall love your neighbor as yourself."

10　Love does no wrong to a neighbor; therefore love is the fulfilling of the law.

11　Besides this you know the time, that the hour has come for you to wake from sleep. For salvation is nearer to us now than when we first believed.

12　The night is far gone; the day is at hand. So then let us cast off the works of darkness and put on the armor* of light.

13　Let us walk properly as in the daytime, not in orgies** and drunkenness, not in sexual immorality and sensuality, not in quarreling and jealousy.

14　But put on the Lord Jesus Christ, and make no provision for the flesh, to gratify its desires.

---

*　armor [ɑ́ːrmər] ⑲ 갑옷.

**　orgy [ɔ́ːrdʒi] ⑲ 먹고 마시며 난잡하게 놀기, 탐닉.

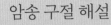

암송 구절 해설

Owe no one anything, except to love each other,
for the one who loves another has fulfilled the law. (13:8)

피차 사랑의 빚 외에는 아무에게든지 아무 빚도 지지 말라
남을 사랑하는 자는 율법을 다 이루었느니라.

남에게 돈이나 물건을 꾸어 쓰는 것을 '빚지다'라고 합니다. 빚을 진 사람들은 갚기 위해 노력합니다. 다 갚아야 빚에서 벗어나 자유를 얻기 때문입니다. 그런데 그리스도인에게는 절대로 갚을 수 없는 빚이 있습니다. '사랑의 빚'입니다. 하나님을 기쁘시게 하기 위해 우리가 해야 할 일은 하나님을 사랑하고 이웃을 사랑하는 것입니다.

✎ 하루 한 문장, 생각 쓰기

오늘 본문을 쓰면서 깨달은 지혜, 새롭게 다짐한 점,
떠오른 생각 등을 자유롭게 적어 보세요.

Romans 14

Do Not Pass Judgment on One Another

1   As for the one who is weak in faith, welcome him, but not to quarrel over opinions.

2   One person believes he may eat anything, while the weak person eats only vegetables.

3   Let not the one who eats despise the one who abstains, and let not the one who abstains pass judgment on the one who eats, for God has welcomed him.

4   Who are you to pass judgment on the servant of another? It is before his own master that he stands or falls. And he will be upheld, for the Lord is able to make him stand.

5   One person esteems one day as better than another, while another esteems all days alike. Each one should be fully convinced in his own mind.

6   The one who observes the day, observes it in honor of the Lord. The one who eats, eats in honor of the Lord, since he gives thanks to God, while the one who abstains, abstains in honor of the Lord and gives thanks to God.

7   For none of us lives to himself, and none of us dies to himself.

8 For if we live, we live to the Lord, and if we die, we die to the Lord. So then, whether we live or whether we die, we are the Lord's.

9 For to this end Christ died and lived again, that he might be Lord both of the dead and of the living.

10 Why do you pass judgment on your brother? Or you, why do you despise your brother? For we will all stand before the judgment seat of God;

11 for it is written, "As I live, says the Lord, every knee shall bow to me, and every tongue shall confess to God."

12 So then each of us will give an account of himself to God.

Do Not Cause Another to Stumble

13 Therefore let us not pass judgment on one another any longer, but rather decide never to put a stumbling block or hindrance in the way of a brother.

14 I know and am persuaded in the Lord Jesus that nothing is unclean in itself, but it is unclean for anyone who thinks it unclean.

15 For if your brother is grieved by what you eat, you are no longer walking in love. By what you eat, do not destroy the one for whom Christ died.

16 So do not let what you regard as good be spoken of as evil.

17 For the kingdom of God is not a matter of eating and drinking but of righteousness and peace and joy in the Holy Spirit.

18 Whoever thus serves Christ is acceptable to God and approved by men.

19 So then let us pursue what makes for peace and for mutual upbuilding.

20 Do not, for the sake of food, destroy the work of God. Everything is indeed clean, but it is wrong for anyone to make another stumble by what he eats.

21 It is good not to eat meat or drink wine or do anything that causes your brother to stumble.

22 The faith that you have, keep between yourself and God. Blessed is the one who has no reason to pass judgment on himself for what he approves.

23 But whoever has doubts is condemned if he eats, because the eating is not from faith. For whatever does not proceed from faith is sin.

암송 구절 해설

For if we live, we live to the Lord, and if we die, we die to the Lord.
So then, whether we live or whether we die, we are the Lord's. (14:8)

우리가 살아도 주를 위하여 살고 죽어도 주를 위하여 죽나니
그러므로 사나 죽으나 우리가 주의 것이로다.

로마 교회 안에서 유대인과 이방인 사이에 음식을 가려 먹는 문제와 절기를 지키는 문제로 갈등이 생겨났습니다. 이렇듯 결정하기 어려운 문제에 직면했을 때 바울이 제시한 해법은 "주를 위하여"입니다. 그리스도인은 오직 하나님 안에서만 자유를 누릴 수 있기 때문입니다.

✎ 하루 한 문장, 생각 쓰기   오늘 본문을 쓰면서 깨달은 지혜, 새롭게 다짐한 점,
떠오른 생각 등을 자유롭게 적어 보세요.

Romans 15

The Example of Christ

1 We who are strong have an obligation* to bear with the failings of the weak, and not to please ourselves.

2 Let each of us please his neighbor for his good, to build him up.

3 For Christ did not please himself, but as it is written, "The reproaches of those who reproached you fell on me."

4 For whatever was written in former days was written for our instruction**, that through endurance and through the encouragement of the Scriptures we might have hope.

5 May the God of endurance and encouragement grant you to live in such harmony with one another, in accord with Christ Jesus,

6 that together you may with one voice glorify the God and Father of our Lord Jesus Christ.

7 Therefore welcome one another as Christ has welcomed you, for the glory of God.

---

*   obligation [ɑːbləgéiʃən] 몡 의무, 책임, 계약.
**   instruction [instrʌkʃən] 몡 지식, 교육, 가르침.

Christ the Hope of Jews and Gentiles

8 For I tell you that Christ became a servant to the circumcised to show God's truthfulness, in order to confirm the promises given to the patriarchs,

9 and in order that the Gentiles might glorify God for his mercy. As it is written, "Therefore I will praise you among the Gentiles, and sing to your name."

10 And again it is said, "Rejoice, O Gentiles, with his people."

11 And again, "Praise the Lord, all you Gentiles, and let all the peoples extol him."

12 And again Isaiah says, "The root of Jesse will come, even he who arises to rule the Gentiles; in him will the Gentiles hope."

13 May the God of hope fill you with all joy and peace in believing, so that by the power of the Holy Spirit you may abound in hope.

Paul the Minister to the Gentiles

14 I myself am satisfied about you, my brothers, that you yourselves are full of goodness, filled with all knowledge and able to instruct one another.

15 But on some points I have written to you very boldly by way of reminder, because of the grace given me by God

16 to be a minister of Christ Jesus to the Gentiles in the priestly service of the gospel of God, so that the offering of the Gentiles may be acceptable, sanctified by the Holy Spirit.

17 In Christ Jesus, then, I have reason to be proud of my work for God.

18 For I will not venture* to speak of anything except what Christ has accomplished through me to bring the Gentiles to obedience—by word and deed,

19 by the power of signs and wonders, by the power of the Spirit of God—so that from Jerusalem and all the way around to Illyricum I have fulfilled the ministry of the gospel of Christ;

20 and thus I make it my ambition to preach the gospel, not where Christ has already been named, lest I build on someone else's foundation,

21 but as it is written, "Those who have never been told of him will see, and those who have never heard will understand."

Paul's Plan to Visit Rome

22 This is the reason why I have so often been hindered from coming to you.

23 But now, since I no longer have any room for work in these regions, and since I have longed for many years to come to you,

24 I hope to see you in passing as I go to Spain, and to be helped on my journey there by you, once I have enjoyed your company for a while.

25 At present, however, I am going to Jerusalem bringing aid to the saints.

26 For Macedonia and Achaia have been pleased to make some contribution for the poor among the saints at Jerusalem.

---

* venture [véntʃər] 몡 모험. 투기적 사업.

27 For they were pleased to do it, and indeed they owe it to them.
For if the Gentiles have come to share in their spiritual blessings,
they ought also to be of service to them in material blessings.

28 When therefore I have completed this and have delivered to them
what has been collected, I will leave for Spain by way of you.

29 I know that when I come to you I will come in the fullness of
the blessing of Christ.

30 I appeal to you, brothers, by our Lord Jesus Christ and by the love
of the Spirit, to strive together with me in your prayers to God on
my behalf,

31 that I may be delivered from the unbelievers in Judea, and that my
service for Jerusalem may be acceptable to the saints,

32 so that by God's will I may come to you with joy and be refreshed
in your company.

33 May the God of peace be with you all. Amen.

암송 구절 해설

Therefore welcome one another
as Christ has welcomed you, for the glory of God. (15:7)

그러므로 그리스도께서 우리를 받아 하나님께 영광을 돌리심과 같이
너희도 서로 받으라.

바울은 로마 교회의 연합을 위해 서로 받으라고 호소합니다. 그리스도인들이 서로 대
립하고 하나 되지 못한다면 세상의 본이 되지 못하여 복음을 전하는 데 방해가 될 뿐
아니라 하나님께 영광을 돌릴 수 없기 때문입니다. 죄인인 우리를 받아 주신 예수님을
본받아 우리도 서로 용납하고 이해하며 하나 되기 위해 노력해야 합니다.

오늘 본문을 쓰면서 깨달은 지혜, 새롭게 다짐한 점.
떠오른 생각 등을 자유롭게 적어 보세요.

Romans 16

Personal Greetings

1   I commend to you our sister Phoebe, a servant of the church at
    Cenchreae,

2   that you may welcome her in the Lord in a way worthy of
    the saints, and help her in whatever she may need from you,
    for she has been a patron* of many and of myself as well.

3   Greet Prisca and Aquila, my fellow workers in Christ Jesus,

4   who risked their necks for my life, to whom not only I give thanks
    but all the churches of the Gentiles give thanks as well.

5   Greet also the church in their house. Greet my beloved Epaenetus,
    who was the first convert to Christ in Asia.

6   Greet Mary, who has worked hard for you.

7   Greet Andronicus and Junia, my kinsmen and my fellow prisoners.
    They are well known to the apostles, and they were in Christ before
    me.

8   Greet Ampliatus, my beloved in the Lord.

9   Greet Urbanus, our fellow worker in Christ, and my beloved
    Stachys.

---

*   patron [péitrən] 명 후원자, 단골.

10 Greet Apelles, who is approved in Christ. Greet those who belong
    to the family of Aristobulus.

11 Greet my kinsman* Herodion. Greet those in the Lord who
    belong to the family of Narcissus.

12 Greet those workers in the Lord, Tryphaena and Tryphosa.
    Greet the beloved Persis, who has worked hard in the Lord.

13 Greet Rufus, chosen in the Lord; also his mother, who has been
    a mother to me as well.

14 Greet Asyncritus, Phlegon, Hermes, Patrobas, Hermas,
    and the brothers who are with them.

15 Greet Philologus, Julia, Nereus and his sister, and Olympas,
    and all the saints who are with them.

16 Greet one another with a holy kiss. All the churches of Christ greet
    you.

Final Instructions and Greetings

17 I appeal to you, brothers, to watch out for those who cause
    divisions and create obstacles contrary to the doctrine that you
    have been taught; avoid them.

18 For such persons do not serve our Lord Christ, but their own
    appetites, and by smooth talk and flattery they deceive the hearts
    of the naive.

19 For your obedience is known to all, so that I rejoice over you,
    but I want you to be wise as to what is good and innocent as to
    what is evil.

---

* kinsman [kinzmən] ⑲ 친척, 동족인 사람.

20 The God of peace will soon crush* Satan under your feet. The grace of our Lord Jesus Christ be with you.

21 Timothy, my fellow worker, greets you; so do Lucius and Jason and Sosipater, my kinsmen.

22 I Tertius, who wrote this letter, greet you in the Lord.

23 Gaius, who is host to me and to the whole church, greets you. Erastus, the city treasurer, and our brother Quartus, greet you.

Doxology

25 Now to him who is able to strengthen you according to my gospel and the preaching of Jesus Christ, according to the revelation of the mystery that was kept secret for long ages

26 but has now been disclosed and through the prophetic** writings has been made known to all nations, according to the command of the eternal God, to bring about the obedience of faith—

27 to the only wise God be glory forevermore*** through Jesus Christ! Amen.

---

*   crush [krʌʃ] ⑧ 부수다, 으깨다, 궤멸시키다.

**   prophetic [prəfétik] ⑩ 예언자의, 예언의.

***   forevermore [fərèvərmɔ́:r] ⑨ 이제부터 영원히

암송 구절 해설

So that I rejoice over you, but I want you to be wise as to what is good
and innocent as to what is evil. (16:19b)

그러므로 내가 너희로 말미암아 기뻐하노니
너희가 선한 데 지혜롭고 악한 데 미련하기를 원하노라.

바울은 분쟁을 일으키거나 잘못된 가르침을 전하는 사람들을 경계하라고 주의를 주면서 선한 데는 지혜롭고 악한 데는 미련하라고 격려합니다. 사탄은 지금도 우리의 믿음을 무너뜨리고 교회를 갈라놓기 위해 애를 씁니다. 오직 진리에 순종할 때 우리는 이런 유혹을 이겨 내고 주님이 주시는 승리를 맛볼 수 있습니다.

오늘 본문을 쓰면서 깨달은 지혜, 새롭게 다짐한 점,
떠오른 생각 등을 자유롭게 적어 보세요.

Hebrews 1

The Supremacy of God's Son

1   Long ago, at many times and in many ways, God spoke to our fathers by the prophets,

2   but in these last days he has spoken to us by his Son, whom he appointed the heir of all things, through whom also he created the world.

3   He is the radiance* of the glory of God and the exact imprint of his nature, and he upholds the universe by the word of his power. After making purification** for sins, he sat down at the right hand of the Majesty on high,

4   having become as much superior to angels as the name he has inherited is more excellent than theirs.

5   For to which of the angels did God ever say, "You are my Son, today I have begotten you"? Or again, "I will be to him a father, and he shall be to me a son"?

6   And again, when he brings the firstborn into the world, he says, "Let all God's angels worship him."

---

*   radiance [réidiəns] ⑲ 광채. 광휘. 찬란한 빛.
** purification [pjùərəfikéiʃən] ⑲ 정화. 정결.

7 Of the angels he says, "He makes his angels winds, and his ministers a flame of fire."

8 But of the Son he says, "Your throne, O God, is forever and ever, the scepter* of uprightness is the scepter of your kingdom.

9 You have loved righteousness and hated wickedness; therefore God, your God, has anointed you with the oil of gladness beyond your companions."

10 And, "You, Lord, laid the foundation of the earth in the beginning, and the heavens are the work of your hands;

11 they will perish, but you remain; they will all wear out like a garment**,

12 like a robe you will roll them up, like a garment they will be changed. But you are the same, and your years will have no end."

13 And to which of the angels has he ever said, "Sit at my right hand until I make your enemies a footstool*** for your feet"?

14 Are they not all ministering spirits sent out to serve for the sake of those who are to inherit salvation?

---

*   scepter [séptər] 몡 규, 옥으로 만든 홀(笏), 왕권.
**   garment [gάːrmənt] 몡 의류, 옷.
*** footstool [futstuːl] 몡 발판.

암송 구절 해설

He is the radiance of the glory of God and the exact imprint of his nature,
and he upholds the universe by the word of his power.
After making purification for sins,
he sat down at the right hand of the Majesty on high. (1:3)

이는 하나님의 영광의 광채시요 그 본체의 형상이시라
그의 능력의 말씀으로 만물을 붙드시며 죄를 정결하게 하는 일을 하시고
높은 곳에 계신 지극히 크신 이의 우편에 앉으셨느니라.

히브리서 1장은 예수 그리스도가 누구이며 왜 탁월한 분인지를 이야기해 줍니다. 예수
님은 하나님의 영광을 드러내는 빛이요 하나님의 본래 모습을 그대로 보여 주는 분입
니다. 그분은 하나님이 지으신 세계를 능력의 말씀으로 붙드시고 보존하시며, 하나님
의 우편에 앉아 영광을 받으십니다.

오늘 본문을 쓰면서 깨달은 지혜, 새롭게 다짐한 점,
떠오른 생각 등을 자유롭게 적어 보세요.

Hebrews 2

Warning Against Neglecting Salvation

1 Therefore we must pay much closer attention to what we have heard, lest we drift* away from it.

2 For since the message declared by angels proved to be reliable, and every transgression or disobedience received a just retribution,

3 how shall we escape if we neglect** such a great salvation? It was declared at first by the Lord, and it was attested to us by those who heard,

4 while God also bore witness by signs and wonders and various miracles and by gifts of the Holy Spirit distributed according to his will.

The Founder of Salvation

5 For it was not to angels that God subjected the world to come, of which we are speaking.

6 It has been testified somewhere, "What is man, that you are mindful of him, or the son of man, that you care for him?

---

*   drift [drift] ⑧ 표류하다, 떠돌다. ⑲ 표류, 위력.

** neglect [niglékt] ⑧ 등한시하다, 무시하다, 소홀히 하다. ⑲ 무시, 태만.

7   You made him for a little while lower than the angels; you have crowned him with glory and honor,

8   putting everything in subjection under his feet." Now in putting everything in subjection to him, he left nothing outside his control. At present, we do not yet see everything in subjection to him.

9   But we see him who for a little while was made lower than the angels, namely Jesus, crowned with glory and honor because of the suffering of death, so that by the grace of God he might taste death for everyone.

10 For it was fitting that he, for whom and by whom all things exist, in bringing many sons to glory, should make the founder of their salvation perfect through suffering.

11 For he who sanctifies and those who are sanctified all have one source. That is why he is not ashamed to call them brothers,

12 saying, "I will tell of your name to my brothers; in the midst of the congregation I will sing your praise."

13 And again, "I will put my trust in him." And again, "Behold, I and the children God has given me."

14 Since therefore the children share in flesh and blood, he himself likewise partook of* the same things, that through death he might destroy the one who has the power of death, that is, the devil,

15 and deliver all those who through fear of death were subject to lifelong slavery.

16 For surely it is not angels that he helps, but he helps the offspring of Abraham.

---

*   partake of ~을 함께 하다.

17 Therefore he had to be made like his brothers in every respect, so that he might become a merciful and faithful high priest* in the service of God, to make propitiation for the sins of the people.

18 <u>For because he himself has suffered when tempted, he is able to help those who are being tempted.</u>

---

*   high priest ⑲ 대제사장, 대사제, 주창자.

암송 구절 해설

For because he himself has suffered when tempted,
he is able to help those who are being tempted. (2:18)

그가 시험을 받아 고난을 당하셨은즉 시험 받는 자들을 능히 도우실 수 있느니라.

예수님은 자비하고 신실한 대제사장이 되셔서 우리의 죄를 대신 씻어 구원해 주셨습니다. 하나님이시면서 또한 인간이신 예수님은 우리의 연약함을 불쌍히 여기시며, 그분이 직접 고난을 당하셨기 때문에 시험을 받는 자들에게 적절한 도움을 주실 수 있습니다.

오늘 본문을 쓰면서 깨달은 지혜, 새롭게 다짐한 점.
떠오른 생각 등을 자유롭게 적어 보세요.

Hebrews 3

Jesus Greater Than Moses

1 Therefore, holy brothers, you who share in a heavenly calling, consider Jesus, the apostle and high priest of our confession*,

2 who was faithful to him who appointed him, just as Moses also was faithful in all God's house.

3 For Jesus has been counted worthy of more glory than Moses— as much more glory as the builder of a house has more honor than the house itself.

4 (For every house is built by someone, but the builder of all things is God.)

5 Now Moses was faithful in all God's house as a servant, to testify** to the things that were to be spoken later,

6 but Christ is faithful over God's house as a son. And we are his house, if indeed we hold fast our confidence and our boasting in our hope.

---

* confession [kənféʃən] 똉 고백, 실토, 고해, 참회.

** testify [téstəfài] 똉 증언하다, 입증하다.

A Rest for the People of God

7   Therefore, as the Holy Spirit says, "Today, if you hear his voice,

8   do not harden your hearts as in the rebellion*, on the day of testing in the wilderness,

9   where your fathers put me to the test and saw my works for forty years.

10 Therefore I was provoked with that generation, and said, 'They always go astray in their heart; they have not known my ways.'

11 As I swore in my wrath, 'They shall not enter my rest.'"

12 Take care, brothers, lest there be in any of you an evil, unbelieving heart, leading you to fall away from the living God.

13 But exhort one another every day, as long as it is called "today," that none of you may be hardened by the deceitfulness of sin.

14 For we have come to share in Christ, if indeed we hold our original confidence firm to the end.

15 As it is said, "Today, if you hear his voice, do not harden your hearts as in the rebellion."

16 For who were those who heard and yet rebelled? Was it not all those who left Egypt led by Moses?

17 And with whom was he provoked for forty years? Was it not with those who sinned, whose bodies fell in the wilderness?

18 And to whom did he swear that they would not enter his rest, but to those who were disobedient?

19 So we see that they were unable to enter because of unbelief.

---

*   rebellion [ribéljən] ⑱ 반란, 반역, 반항.

암송 구절 해설

For we have come to share in Christ,
if indeed we hold our original confidence firm to the end. (3:14)

우리가 시작할 때에 확신한 것을 끝까지 견고히 잡고 있으면
그리스도와 함께 참여한 자가 되리라.

'확신한 것'은 그리스도를 믿는 믿음을 가리킵니다. 오직 진정으로 회심하고 그리스도
께 속한 사람만이 세상의 유혹에 넘어가지 않고 끝까지 인내하면서 믿음을 견고하게
붙잡을 수 있습니다. 그럴 때 우리는 그리스도와 함께, 그분이 하시는 모든 일에 참여
할 수 있습니다.

오늘 본문을 쓰면서 깨달은 지혜, 새롭게 다짐한 점,
떠오른 생각 등을 자유롭게 적어 보세요.

Hebrews 4

1   Therefore, while the promise of entering his rest still stands,
    let us fear lest any of you should seem to have failed to reach it.

2   For good news came to us just as to them, but the message they
    heard did not benefit them, because they were not united by faith
    with those who listened.

3   For we who have believed enter that rest, as he has said,
    "As I swore in my wrath, 'They shall not enter my rest,'" although
    his works were finished from the foundation of the world.

4   For he has somewhere spoken of the seventh day in this way:
    "And God rested on the seventh day from all his works."

5   And again in this passage* he said, "They shall not enter my rest."

6   Since therefore it remains for some to enter it, and those who
    formerly received the good news failed to enter because of
    disobedience,

7   again he appoints a certain day, "Today," saying through David so
    long afterward, in the words already quoted, "Today, if you hear
    his voice, do not harden your hearts."

8   For if Joshua had given them rest, God would not have spoken of
    another day later on.

*   passage [pǽsidʒ] ⑲ 통로, 구절, 통과. ⑧ 가로지르다, 통과하다.

9   So then, there remains a Sabbath* rest for the people of God,

10 for whoever has entered God's rest has also rested from his works
    as God did from his.

11 Let us therefore strive to enter that rest, so that no one may fall by
    the same sort of disobedience.

12 For the word of God is living and active, sharper than any
    two-edged sword, piercing** to the division of soul and of spirit,
    of joints and of marrow, and discerning the thoughts and
    intentions of the heart.

13 And no creature is hidden from his sight, but all are naked and
    exposed to the eyes of him to whom we must give account.

Jesus the Great High Priest

14 Since then we have a great high priest who has passed through
    the heavens, Jesus, the Son of God, let us hold fast our confession.

15 For we do not have a high priest who is unable to sympathize with
    our weaknesses, but one who in every respect has been tempted as
    we are, yet without sin.

16 Let us then with confidence draw near to the throne of grace,
    that we may receive mercy and find grace to help in time of need.

---

*   Sabbath [sǽbəθ] ⑲ 안식일. 유대교에서 금요일 해질 때부터 토요일 해질 때까지를 이르는 말이며,
     이날은 모든 일을 하지 않고 휴식을 취한다.
** pierce [píərsiŋ] ⑧ 찌르다, 꿰뚫다, 관통하다.

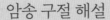

암송 구절 해설

Let us then with confidence draw near to the throne of grace,
that we may receive mercy and find grace to help in time of need. (4:16)

그러므로 우리는 긍휼하심을 받고 때를 따라 돕는 은혜를 얻기 위하여
은혜의 보좌 앞에 담대히 나아갈 것이니라.

'담대히' 나아갈 수 있다는 말은 우리가 죄 때문에 벌을 받을까 두려워하지 않고 우리 모습 그대로 숨김없이 하나님 앞에 갈 수 있다는 뜻입니다. 예수님은 우리의 연약함을 동정하시며 우리와 똑같이 시험을 받으신 분이기 때문에 우리는 은혜의 보좌 앞으로 담대히 나아갈 수 있습니다.

Hebrews 5

1 For every high priest chosen from among men is appointed to act on behalf of men in relation to God, to offer gifts and sacrifices for sins.

2 He can deal gently with the ignorant and wayward, since he himself is beset with weakness.

3 Because of this he is obligated to offer sacrifice for his own sins just as he does for those of the people.

4 And no one takes this honor for himself, but only when called by God, just as Aaron was.

5 So also Christ did not exalt himself to be made a high priest, but was appointed by him who said to him, "You are my Son, today I have begotten you";

6 as he says also in another place, "You are a priest forever, after the order of Melchizedek*."

7 In the days of his flesh, Jesus offered up prayers and supplications, with loud cries and tears, to him who was able to save him from death, and he was heard because of his reverence.

8 Although he was a son, he learned obedience through what he suffered.

---

* the order of Melchizedek 멜기세덱의 반차. 예수님의 신적 기원을 설명할 때 사용한 표현.

9　And being made perfect, he became the source of eternal salvation to all who obey him,

10　being designated by God a high priest after the order of Melchizedek.

Warning Against Apostasy

11　About this we have much to say, and it is hard to explain, since you have become dull of hearing.

12　For though by this time you ought to be teachers, you need someone to teach you again the basic principles of the oracles of God. You need milk, not solid food,

13　for everyone who lives on milk is unskilled in the word of righteousness, since he is a child.

14　But solid food is for the mature, for those who have their powers of discernment trained by constant practice to distinguish good from evil.

암송 구절 해설

Although he was a son, he learned obedience through what he suffered.
And being made perfect, he became the source of eternal salvation
to all who obey him. (5:8-9)

그가 아들이시면서도 받으신 고난으로 순종함을 배워서 온전하게 되셨은즉
자기에게 순종하는 모든 자에게 영원한 구원의 근원이 되시고.

예수님은 하나님의 아들이지만, 이 땅에서 인간으로 살아가면서 하나님의 뜻을 행할
때 뒤따르는 고난을 고스란히 받으셨습니다. 이를 통해 하나님께 순종한다는 의미가
무엇인지를 배우고 온전해지심으로 '영원한 구원의 근원'이 되셨습니다.

오늘 본문을 쓰면서 깨달은 지혜, 새롭게 다짐한 점,
떠오른 생각 등을 자유롭게 적어 보세요.

Hebrews 6

1 Therefore let us leave the elementary doctrine of Christ and go on to maturity, not laying again a foundation of repentance from dead works and of faith toward God,

2 and of instruction about washings, the laying on of hands, the resurrection of the dead, and eternal judgment.

3 And this we will do if God permits.

4 For it is impossible, in the case of those who have once been enlightened, who have tasted the heavenly gift, and have shared in the Holy Spirit,

5 and have tasted the goodness of the word of God and the powers of the age to come,

6 and then have fallen away, to restore them again to repentance, since they are crucifying once again the Son of God to their own harm and holding him up to contempt.

7 For land that has drunk the rain that often falls on it, and produces a crop useful to those for whose sake it is cultivated, receives a blessing from God.

8 But if it bears thorns and thistles*, it is worthless and near to being cursed, and its end is to be burned.

---

* thistle [θísl] ⑲ 엉겅퀴.

9 Though we speak in this way, yet in your case, beloved,
   we feel sure of better things—things that belong to salvation.

10 For God is not unjust so as to overlook your work and the love
   that you have shown for his name in serving the saints, as you still
   do.

11 And we desire each one of you to show the same earnestness to
   have the full assurance of hope until the end,

12 so that you may not be sluggish*, but imitators of those who
   through faith and patience inherit the promises.

The Certainty of God's Promise

13 For when God made a promise to Abraham, since he had no one
   greater by whom to swear, he swore by himself,

14 saying, "Surely I will bless you and multiply you."

15 And thus Abraham, having patiently waited, obtained the promise.

16 For people swear by something greater than themselves, and in all
   their disputes an oath is final for confirmation.

17 So when God desired to show more convincingly to the heirs of
   the promise the unchangeable character of his purpose,
   he guaranteed it with an oath,

18 so that by two unchangeable things, in which it is impossible for
   God to lie, we who have fled for refuge might have strong
   encouragement to hold fast to the hope set before us.

---

* sluggish [slʌgiʃ] ⑱ 게으른, 느린, 부진한.

19 We have this as a sure and steadfast* anchor** of the soul, a hope
    that enters into the inner place behind the curtain,

20 where Jesus has gone as a forerunner*** on our behalf, having
    become a high priest forever after the order of Melchizedek.

---

*   steadfast [stédfæst] ⑱ 확고한, 견실한, 고정된.

**   anchor [ǽŋkər] ⑲ 닻, 고정 장치, 앵커. ⑧ 고정시키다, 닻을 내리다.

***   forerunner [fɔ́rənər] ⑱ 선인, 선조, 선구자.

암송 구절 해설

And thus Abraham, having patiently waited, obtained the promise. (6:15)

그가 이같이 오래 참아 약속을 받았느니라.

하나님은 아브라함에게 그의 자손을 번성하게 하겠다고 약속하셨습니다. 아브라함은
하나님을 믿고 오랫동안 인내했으며, 마침내 약속의 자손을 얻었습니다. 이처럼 그리
스도인이 소망을 가지고 세상을 살아가게 해 주는 힘은 부유한 환경이나 뛰어난 능력
이 아니라 하나님의 약속에 있습니다.

오늘 본문을 쓰면서 깨달은 지혜, 새롭게 다짐한 점,
떠오른 생각 등을 자유롭게 적어 보세요.

Hebrews 7

The Priestly Order of Melchizedek

1   For this Melchizedek, king of Salem, priest of the Most High God, met Abraham returning from the slaughter of the kings and blessed him,

2   and to him Abraham apportioned a tenth part of everything. He is first, by translation of his name, king of righteousness, and then he is also king of Salem, that is, king of peace.

3   He is without father or mother or genealogy*, having neither beginning of days nor end of life, but resembling the Son of God he continues a priest forever.

4   See how great this man was to whom Abraham the patriarch gave a tenth of the spoils!

5   And those descendants of Levi who receive the priestly office have a commandment in the law to take tithes** from the people, that is, from their brothers, though these also are descended from Abraham.

---

*   genealogy [dʒìːniǽlədʒi] ⑱ 계보, 혈통, 족보.

**   tithe [taið] ⑱ 십일조, 10분의 1.

6   But this man who does not have his descent from them received
    tithes from Abraham and blessed him who had the promises.

7   It is beyond dispute that the inferior is blessed by the superior.

8   In the one case tithes are received by mortal men, but in the other
    case, by one of whom it is testified that he lives.

9   One might even say that Levi himself, who receives tithes, paid
    tithes through Abraham,

10 for he was still in the loins of his ancestor when Melchizedek met
    him.

Jesus Compared to Melchizedek

11 Now if perfection had been attainable through the Levitical*
    priesthood** (for under it the people received the law), what further
    need would there have been for another priest to arise after
    the order of Melchizedek, rather than one named after the order of
    Aaron?

12 For when there is a change in the priesthood, there is necessarily
    a change in the law as well.

13 For the one of whom these things are spoken belonged to another
    tribe, from which no one has ever served at the altar.

14 For it is evident that our Lord was descended from Judah,
    and in connection with that tribe Moses said nothing about priests.

15 This becomes even more evident when another priest arises
    in the likeness of Melchizedek,

---

*   Levitical [livítikəl] ⑬ 레위 사람의, 레위족의.
**   priesthood [prísthʊd] ⑬ 성직, 사제직

16 who has become a priest, not on the basis of a legal requirement concerning bodily descent, but by the power of an indestructible* life.

17 For it is witnessed of him, "You are a priest forever, after the order of Melchizedek."

18 For on the one hand, a former commandment is set aside because of its weakness and uselessness

19 (for the law made nothing perfect); but on the other hand, a better hope is introduced, through which we draw near to God.

20 And it was not without an oath. For those who formerly became priests were made such without an oath,

21 but this one was made a priest with an oath by the one who said to him: "The Lord has sworn and will not change his mind, 'You are a priest forever.'"

22 This makes Jesus the guarantor** of a better covenant.

23 The former priests were many in number, because they were prevented by death from continuing in office,

24 but he holds his priesthood permanently***, because he continues forever.

25 Consequently, he is able to save to the uttermost those who draw near to God through him, since he always lives to make intercession for them.

---

*   indestructible [indistrʌktəbl] ⑱ 파괴할 수 없는, 불멸의.
** guarantor [gǽrəntɔ̀:r] ⑲ 보증인, 인수인.
*** permanently [pə́:rmənəntli] ⑲ 영원히, 영구적으로.

26 For it was indeed fitting that we should have such a high priest,
holy, innocent, unstained*, separated from sinners, and exalted
above the heavens.

27 He has no need, like those high priests, to offer sacrifices daily,
first for his own sins and then for those of the people, since he did
this once for all when he offered up himself.

28 For the law appoints men in their weakness as high priests,
but the word of the oath, which came later than the law, appoints
a Son who has been made perfect forever.

---

*   unstained [ʌnstéind] ⑱ 흠 없는, 도덕적 결점이 없는.

암송 구절 해설

For it was indeed fitting that we should have such a high priest, holy, innocent,
unstained, separated from sinners, and exalted above the heavens. (7:26)

이러한 대제사장은 우리에게 합당하니 거룩하고 악이 없고 더러움이 없고
죄인에게서 떠나 계시고 하늘보다 높이 되신 이라.

여기에서 '대제사장'은 예수 그리스도를 가리킵니다. '거룩'은 하나님을 경배하고 기쁘
시게 한다는 뜻입니다. '악이 없고'는 사람들에게 상처를 입히거나 악영향을 끼치지 않
았다는 뜻입니다. '더러움이 없고'는 사람들과 어울렸지만 때가 묻지 않음을 가리킵니
다. 예수님은 이러한 대제사장이기에 하늘보다 높이 되셨고, 우리의 필요를 채워 주실
수 있습니다.

오늘 본문을 쓰면서 깨달은 지혜, 새롭게 다짐한 점,
떠오른 생각 등을 자유롭게 적어 보세요.

Hebrews 8

Jesus, High Priest of a Better Covenant

1   Now the point in what we are saying is this: we have such
    a high priest, one who is seated at the right hand of the throne of
    the Majesty in heaven,

2   a minister in the holy places, in the true tent that the Lord set up,
    not man.

3   For every high priest is appointed to offer gifts and sacrifices;
    thus it is necessary for this priest also to have something to offer.

4   Now if he were on earth, he would not be a priest at all,
    since there are priests who offer gifts according to the law.

5   They serve a copy and shadow of the heavenly things.
    For when Moses was about to erect* the tent, he was instructed**
    by God, saying, "See that you make everything according to
    the pattern that was shown you on the mountain."

6   But as it is, Christ has obtained a ministry that is as much more
    excellent than the old as the covenant he mediates is better,
    since it is enacted on better promises.

---

*   erect [irékt] ⑧ 세우다, 짓다. ⑱ 곤두선, 곧은.
**   enact [inǽkt] ⑧ 제정하다, 시행하다, 일으키다.

7　For if that first covenant had been faultless*, there would have been no occasion to look for a second.

8　For he finds fault with them when he says: "Behold, the days are coming, declares the Lord, when I will establish a new covenant with the house of Israel and with the house of Judah,

9　not like the covenant that I made with their fathers on the day when I took them by the hand to bring them out of the land of Egypt. For they did not continue in my covenant, and so I showed no concern for them, declares the Lord.

10　For this is the covenant that I will make with the house of Israel after those days, declares the Lord: I will put my laws into their minds, and write them on their hearts, and I will be their God, and they shall be my people.

11　And they shall not teach, each one his neighbor and each one his brother, saying, 'Know the Lord,' for they shall all know me, from the least of them to the greatest.

12　For I will be merciful toward their iniquities, and I will remember their sins no more."

13　In speaking of a new covenant, he makes the first one obsolete**. And what is becoming obsolete and growing old is ready to vanish away.

---

*　faultless [fɔ́:ltlis] ⑱ 결점 없는, 완전한, 나무랄 데 없는.

**　obsolete [ὰbsəlíːt] ⑱ 쇠퇴한, 구식의, 쓸모없게 된.

암송 구절 해설

But as it is, Christ has obtained a ministry that is as much more excellent
than the old as the covenant he mediates is better,
since it is enacted on better promises. (8:6)

그러나 이제 그는 더 아름다운 직분을 얻으셨으니
그는 더 좋은 약속으로 세우신 더 좋은 언약의 중보자시라.

6절에서 이야기하는 언약은 구약 시대 때 이스라엘 백성과 맺은 옛 언약보다 '더 좋은
언약'입니다. '더 좋은 약속'으로 세워진 언약이기 때문입니다. 하나님께서 새 언약을
세우셨기에 우리는 하나님의 백성이 되었고, 예수 그리스도를 통해 하나님 앞으로 직
접 나아갈 수 있게 되었습니다.

오늘 본문을 쓰면서 깨달은 지혜, 새롭게 다짐한 점.
떠오른 생각 등을 자유롭게 적어 보세요.

Hebrews 9

The Earthly Holy Place

1   Now even the first covenant had regulations* for worship and an earthly place of holiness.

2   For a tent was prepared, the first section, in which were the lampstand and the table and the bread of the Presence. It is called the Holy Place.

3   Behind the second curtain was a second section called the Most Holy Place,

4   having the golden altar of incense and the ark of the covenant covered on all sides with gold, in which was a golden urn** holding the manna, and Aaron's staff that budded, and the tablets of the covenant.

5   Above it were the cherubim of glory overshadowing*** the mercy seat. Of these things we cannot now speak in detail.

6   These preparations having thus been made, the priests go regularly into the first section, performing their ritual duties,

---

*   regulation [règjuléiʃən] ⑲ 규정, 법규, 규칙, 조절.

**   urn [əːrn] ⑲ 단지, 항아리, 주전자.

***   overshadow [oúvərʃædou] ⑤ 가리다, 덮다, 흐리게 하다.

7   but into the second only the high priest goes, and he but once
    a year, and not without taking blood, which he offers for himself
    and for the unintentional* sins of the people.

8   By this the Holy Spirit indicates that the way into the holy places
    is not yet opened as long as the first section is still standing

9   (which is symbolic for the present age). According to this
    arrangement, gifts and sacrifices are offered that cannot perfect
    the conscience of the worshiper,

10 but deal only with food and drink and various washings,
    regulations for the body imposed until the time of reformation.

Redemption Through the Blood of Christ

11 But when Christ appeared as a high priest of the good things that
    have come, then through the greater and more perfect tent (not
    made with hands, that is, not of this creation)

12 he entered once for all into the holy places, not by means of
    the blood of goats and calves but by means of his own blood,
    thus securing an eternal redemption.

13 For if the blood of goats and bulls, and the sprinkling of defiled
    persons with the ashes of a heifer, sanctify for the purification of
    the flesh,

14 how much more will the blood of Christ, who through the eternal
    Spirit offered himself without blemish** to God, purify our
    conscience from dead works to serve the living God.

---

*   unintentional [əninténʃənəl] ⑧ 본의 아닌, 무심코, 고의 아닌.
**   blemish [blémiʃ] ⑧ 흠, 결점. ⑧ 손상하다. 더럽히다.

15 Therefore he is the mediator* of a new covenant, so that those who are called may receive the promised eternal inheritance, since a death has occurred that redeems them from the transgressions committed under the first covenant.

16 For where a will is involved, the death of the one who made it must be established.

17 For a will takes effect only at death, since it is not in force as long as the one who made it is alive.

18 Therefore not even the first covenant was inaugurated** without blood.

19 For when every commandment of the law had been declared by Moses to all the people, he took the blood of calves and goats, with water and scarlet wool and hyssop, and sprinkled both the book itself and all the people,

20 saying, "This is the blood of the covenant that God commanded for you."

21 And in the same way he sprinkled with the blood both the tent and all the vessels used in worship.

22 Indeed, under the law almost everything is purified with blood, and without the shedding of blood there is no forgiveness of sins.

23 Thus it was necessary for the copies of the heavenly things to be purified with these rites, but the heavenly things themselves with better sacrifices than these.

---

*   mediator [míːdièitər] ⑱ 중재자, 조정자.

**   inaugurate [inɔ́ːgjurèit] ⑤ 창시하다, 시작하다.

24 For Christ has entered, not into holy places made with hands, which are copies of the true things, but into heaven itself, now to appear in the presence of* God on our behalf.

25 Nor was it to offer himself repeatedly, as the high priest enters the holy places every year with blood not his own,

26 for then he would have had to suffer repeatedly since the foundation of the world. But as it is, he has appeared once for all at the end of the ages to put away sin by the sacrifice of himself.

27 And just as it is appointed for man to die once, and after that comes judgment,

28 so Christ, having been offered once to bear the sins of many, will appear a second time, not to deal with** sin but to save those who are eagerly waiting for him.

---

*   in the presence of ∼의 앞에서, ∼에 직면하여.

**   deal with 다루다, 대하다, 처리하다.

암송 구절 해설

And just as it is appointed for man to die once,
and after that comes judgment. (9:27)

한 번 죽는 것은 사람에게 정해진 것이요 그 후에는 심판이 있으리니.

우리에게는 단 한 번의 삶만 허락되었습니다. 죽음을 피할 수 있는 사람은 아무도 없습니다. 죽음 이후에는 심판이 기다리고 있습니다. 하지만 그리스도인은 심판을 두려워할 이유가 없습니다. 예수님께서 단 한 번의 제사로 우리의 죄를 씻으시고 우리를 구원하시며, 거룩한 백성으로 삼아 주셨기 때문입니다.

오늘 본문을 쓰면서 깨달은 지혜. 새롭게 다짐한 점.
떠오른 생각 등을 자유롭게 적어 보세요.

Hebrews 10

Christ's Sacrifice Once for All

1   For since the law has but a shadow of the good things to come instead of the true form of these realities, it can never, by the same sacrifices that are continually offered every year, make perfect those who draw near.

2   Otherwise, would they not have ceased* to be offered, since the worshipers, having once been cleansed, would no longer have any consciousness** of sins?

3   But in these sacrifices there is a reminder of sins every year.

4   For it is impossible for the blood of bulls and goats to take away sins.

5   Consequently, when Christ came into the world, he said, "Sacrifices and offerings you have not desired, but a body have you prepared for me;

6   in burnt offerings and sin offerings you have taken no pleasure.

7   Then I said, 'Behold, I have come to do your will, O God, as it is written of me in the scroll of the book.'"

---

*   cease [siːs] ⑧ 그치다, 그만두다, 종지부를 찍다.

**   consciousness [kάnʃəsnis] ⑲ 의식, 인식, 정신.

8   When he said above, "You have neither desired nor taken pleasure in sacrifices and offerings and burnt offerings and sin offerings" (these are offered according to the law),

9   then he added, "Behold, I have come to do your will."
He does away with the first in order to establish the second.

10 And by that will we have been sanctified through the offering of the body of Jesus Christ once for all.

11 And every priest stands daily at his service, offering repeatedly the same sacrifices, which can never take away sins.

12 But when Christ had offered for all time a single sacrifice for sins, he sat down at the right hand of God,

13 waiting from that time until his enemies should be made a footstool for his feet.

14 For by a single offering he has perfected for all time those who are being sanctified.

15 And the Holy Spirit also bears witness to us; for after saying,

16 "This is the covenant that I will make with them after those days, declares the Lord: I will put my laws on their hearts, and write them on their minds,"

17 then he adds, "I will remember their sins and their lawless deeds no more."

18 Where there is forgiveness of these, there is no longer any offering for sin.

The Full Assurance of Faith

19 Therefore, brothers, since we have confidence to enter the holy places by the blood of Jesus,

20 by the new and living way that he opened for us through the curtain, that is, through his flesh,

21 and since we have a great priest over the house of God,

22 let us draw near with a true heart in full assurance* of faith, with our hearts sprinkled clean from an evil conscience and our bodies washed with pure water.

23 Let us hold fast the confession of our hope without wavering**, for he who promised is faithful.

24 And let us consider how to stir up one another to love and good works,

25 not neglecting to meet together, as is the habit of some, but encouraging one another, and all the more as you see the Day drawing near.

26 For if we go on sinning deliberately*** after receiving the knowledge of the truth, there no longer remains a sacrifice for sins,

27 but a fearful expectation of judgment, and a fury of fire that will consume the adversaries.

28 Anyone who has set aside the law of Moses dies without mercy on the evidence of two or three witnesses.

---

*　assurance [əʃúərəns] ⑲ 보증, 확신, 확언.

**　wavering [wéivəriŋ] ⑲ 흔들리는, 떨리는.

***　deliberately [dilíbərətli] ⑭ 고의로, 신중히.

29 How much worse punishment, do you think, will be deserved by the one who has trampled* underfoot the Son of God, and has profaned** the blood of the covenant by which he was sanctified, and has outraged the Spirit of grace?

30 For we know him who said, "Vengeance is mine; I will repay." And again, "The Lord will judge his people."

31 It is a fearful thing to fall into the hands of the living God.

32 But recall the former days when, after you were enlightened, you endured a hard struggle with sufferings,

33 sometimes being publicly exposed to reproach and affliction, and sometimes being partners with those so treated.

34 For you had compassion on those in prison, and you joyfully accepted the plundering of your property, since you knew that you yourselves had a better possession and an abiding one.

35 Therefore do not throw away your confidence, which has a great reward.

36 For you have need of endurance, so that when you have done the will of God you may receive what is promised.

37 For, "Yet a little while, and the coming one will come and will not delay;

38 but my righteous one shall live by faith, and if he shrinks back, my soul has no pleasure in him."

39 But we are not of those who shrink back and are destroyed, but of those who have faith and preserve their souls.

---

* trample [trǽmpl] ⑧ 짓밟다, 무시하다.

** profane [prəféin] ⑧ 신을 욕되게 하는, 불경스러운, 세속적인.

암송 구절 해설

But we are not of those who shrink back and are destroyed,
but of those who have faith and preserve their souls. (10:39)

우리는 뒤로 물러가 멸망할 자가 아니요
오직 영혼을 구원함에 이르는 믿음을 가진 자니라.

로마서 1장 17절과 히브리서 10장 38절이 이야기하는 것처럼 의인은 오직 믿음으로
말미암아 살아가는 사람들입니다. 믿음으로 말미암아 산다는 것은 예수 그리스도를
의지하고 인내함으로 우리의 의무를 감당하는 것입니다. 참된 믿음을 가진 사람은 뒤
로 물러나 멸망하지 않으며 예수님이 재림하셨을 때 영생을 얻게 될 것을 확신합니다.

오늘 본문을 쓰면서 깨달은 지혜, 새롭게 다짐한 점.
떠오른 생각 등을 자유롭게 적어 보세요.

Hebrews 11

By Faith

1   Now faith is the assurance of things hoped for, the conviction* of things not seen.

2   For by it the people of old received their commendation.

3   By faith we understand that the universe was created by the word of God, so that what is seen was not made out of things that are visible.

4   By faith Abel offered to God a more acceptable sacrifice than Cain, through which he was commended as righteous, God commending him by accepting his gifts. And through his faith, though he died, he still speaks.

5   By faith Enoch was taken up so that he should not see death, and he was not found, because God had taken him. Now before he was taken he was commended as having pleased God.

6   And without faith it is impossible to please him, for whoever would draw near to God must believe that he exists and that he rewards those who seek him.

---

*   conviction [kənvíkʃən] 명 확신, 유죄 판결.

7   By faith Noah, being warned by God concerning events as yet unseen, in reverent fear constructed an ark for the saving of his household. By this he condemned the world and became an heir of the righteousness that comes by faith.

8   By faith Abraham obeyed when he was called to go out to a place that he was to receive as an inheritance. And he went out, not knowing where he was going.

9   By faith he went to live in the land of promise, as in a foreign land, living in tents with Isaac and Jacob, heirs with him of the same promise.

10 For he was looking forward to the city that has foundations, whose designer and builder is God.

11 By faith Sarah herself received power to conceive, even when she was past the age, since she considered him faithful who had promised.

12 Therefore from one man, and him as good as dead, were born descendants as many as the stars of heaven and as many as the innumerable* grains of sand by the seashore**.

13 These all died in faith, not having received the things promised, but having seen them and greeted them from afar, and having acknowledged that they were strangers and exiles on the earth.

14 For people who speak thus make it clear that they are seeking a homeland.

15 If they had been thinking of that land from which they had gone out, they would have had opportunity to return.

---

*   innumerable [injúːmərəbl] ⓐ 셀 수 없는, 무수한.
** seashore [síːʃɔːr] ⓝ 해변, 바닷가, 해안.

16 But as it is, they desire a better country, that is, a heavenly one. Therefore God is not ashamed to be called their God, for he has prepared for them a city.

17 By faith Abraham, when he was tested, offered up Isaac, and he who had received the promises was in the act of* offering up his only son,

18 of whom it was said, "Through Isaac shall your offspring be named."

19 He considered that God was able even to raise him from the dead, from which, figuratively speaking, he did receive him back.

20 By faith Isaac invoked future blessings on Jacob and Esau.

21 By faith Jacob, when dying, blessed each of the sons of Joseph, bowing in worship over the head of his staff.

22 By faith Joseph, at the end of his life, made mention of the exodus** of the Israelites and gave directions concerning his bones.

23 By faith Moses, when he was born, was hidden for three months by his parents, because they saw that the child was beautiful, and they were not afraid of the king's edict.

24 By faith Moses, when he was grown up, refused to be called the son of Pharaoh's daughter,

25 choosing rather to be mistreated with the people of God than to enjoy the fleeting pleasures of sin.

26 He considered the reproach of Christ greater wealth than the treasures of Egypt, for he was looking to the reward.

---

* in the act of ~ 하고 있는 중에, 막 ~ 하려고 하여.

** exodus [éksədəs] ⑲ 출국, 이주, 출애굽기.

27 By faith he left Egypt, not being afraid of the anger of the king, for he endured as seeing him who is invisible.

28 By faith he kept the Passover* and sprinkled the blood, so that the Destroyer of the firstborn might not touch them.

29 By faith the people crossed the Red Sea as on dry land, but the Egyptians, when they attempted to do the same, were drowned.

30 By faith the walls of Jericho fell down after they had been encircled for seven days.

31 By faith Rahab the prostitute** did not perish with those who were disobedient, because she had given a friendly welcome to the spies.

32 And what more shall I say? For time would fail me to tell of Gideon, Barak, Samson, Jephthah, of David and Samuel and the prophets—

33 who through faith conquered kingdoms, enforced justice, obtained promises, stopped the mouths of lions,

34 quenched the power of fire, escaped the edge of the sword, were made strong out of weakness, became mighty in war, put foreign armies to flight.

35 Women received back their dead by resurrection. Some were tortured, refusing to accept release, so that they might rise again to a better life.

36 Others suffered mocking and flogging***, and even chains and imprisonment.

---

*   Passover [pǽsouvər] ⑲ 유월절(이스라엘 민족이 이집트에서 탈출한 일을 기념하는 축제일).

**   prostitute [prɑ́stətjùːt] ⑲ 매춘부, 기생.

*** flogging [flɑ́giŋ] ⑲ 매질, 채찍질.

37 They were stoned, they were sawn in two, they were killed with the sword. They went about in skins of sheep and goats, destitute*, afflicted**, mistreated—

38 of whom the world was not worthy—wandering about in deserts and mountains, and in dens*** and caves of the earth.

39 And all these, though commended through their faith, did not receive what was promised,

40 since God had provided something better for us, that apart from us they should not be made perfect.

* destitute [déstətjùːt] ⑱ 가난한. 극빈한.
** afflicted [əflíktid] ⑱ 고통을 받는. 괴로워하는.
*** den [den] ⑲ 굴. 동굴. ⑧ 동굴에 살다. 은둔하다.

암송 구절 해설

Now faith is the assurance of things hoped for,
the conviction of things not seen. (11:1)
믿음은 바라는 것들의 실상이요 보이지 않는 것들의 증거니.

이 구절은 믿음의 특징을 이야기합니다. 첫째, 믿음은 그리스도의 재림이나 죽은 자들의 부활과 같이 우리가 바라는 미래 사건의 실체입니다. 둘째, 믿음은 죄 사함이나 우리 안에 거하시는 성령, 우리를 위해 기도하시는 그리스도, 하나님께 가까이 나아가는 것 등 눈에 보이지 않는 것들을 믿도록 설득하는 증거입니다. 그리스도인은 이러한 믿음으로 살아가는 사람들입니다.

✏️ 하루 한 문장, 생각 쓰기

Hebrews 12

Jesus, Founder and Perfecter of Our Faith

1 Therefore, since we are surrounded by so great a cloud of witnesses, let us also lay aside every weight, and sin which clings so closely, and let us run with endurance the race that is set before us,

2 looking to Jesus, the founder and perfecter of our faith, who for the joy that was set before him endured the cross, despising the shame, and is seated at the right hand of the throne of God.

Do Not Grow Weary

3 Consider him who endured from sinners such hostility against himself, so that you may not grow weary or fainthearted.

4 In your struggle against sin you have not yet resisted to the point of shedding your blood.

5 And have you forgotten the exhortation that addresses you as sons? "My son, do not regard lightly the discipline* of the Lord, nor be weary when reproved by him.

6 For the Lord disciplines the one he loves, and chastises** every son whom he receives."

---

*   discipline [dísəplin] ⑲ 훈련, 훈육, 징계. ⑤ 훈련하다, 징계하다.
** chastise [ʧæstáiz] ⑤ 혼을 내다, 책망하다.

7   It is for discipline that you have to endure. God is treating you as sons. For what son is there whom his father does not discipline?

8   If you are left without discipline, in which all have participated, then you are illegitimate* children and not sons.

9   Besides this, we have had earthly fathers who disciplined us and we respected them. Shall we not much more be subject to the Father of spirits and live?

10 For they disciplined us for a short time as it seemed best to them, but he disciplines us for our good, that we may share his holiness.

11 For the moment all discipline seems painful rather than pleasant, but later it yields the peaceful fruit of righteousness to those who have been trained by it.

12 Therefore lift your drooping** hands and strengthen your weak knees,

13 and make straight paths for your feet, so that what is lame may not be put out of joint but rather be healed.

14 Strive for peace with everyone, and for the holiness without which no one will see the Lord.

15 See to it that no one fails to obtain the grace of God; that no "root of bitterness" springs up and causes trouble, and by it many become defiled;

16 that no one is sexually immoral or unholy like Esau, who sold his birthright for a single meal.

---

*   illegitimate [ilidʒítəmət] 몡 사생아, 휑 사생아로 태어난, 불법의.
**   drooping [drú:piŋ] 휑 늘어진, 고개 숙인, 풀이 죽은.

17 For you know that afterward, when he desired to inherit
the blessing, he was rejected, for he found no chance to repent,
though he sought it with tears.

A Kingdom That Cannot Be Shaken

18 For you have not come to what may be touched, a blazing* fire
and darkness and gloom and a tempest

19 and the sound of a trumpet and a voice whose words made
the hearers beg that no further messages be spoken to them.

20 For they could not endure the order that was given, "If even
a beast touches the mountain, it shall be stoned."

21 Indeed, so terrifying was the sight that Moses said, "I tremble with
fear."

22 But you have come to Mount Zion and to the city of the living
God, the heavenly Jerusalem, and to innumerable angels in festal
gathering,

23 and to the assembly of the firstborn who are enrolled in heaven,
and to God, the judge of all, and to the spirits of the righteous
made perfect,

24 and to Jesus, the mediator of a new covenant, and to the sprinkled
blood that speaks a better word than the blood of Abel.

25 See that you do not refuse him who is speaking. For if they did not
escape when they refused him who warned them on earth, much
less will we escape if we reject him who warns from heaven.

---

* blazing [bléiziŋ] ⓗ 불타는, 선명한, 타는 듯한.

DAY 28

26 At that time his voice shook the earth, but now he has promised, "Yet once more I will shake not only the earth but also the heavens."

27 This phrase, "Yet once more," indicates the removal of things that are shaken—that is, things that have been made—in order that the things that cannot be shaken may remain.

28 Therefore let us be grateful for receiving a kingdom that cannot be shaken, and thus let us offer to God acceptable worship, with reverence and awe,

29 for our God is a consuming fire.

암송 구절 해설

Therefore, since we are surrounded by so great a cloud of witnesses,
let us also lay aside every weight, and sin which clings so closely,
and let us run with endurance the race that is set before us,
looking to Jesus, the founder and perfecter of our faith. (12:1-2a)

이러므로 우리에게 구름같이 둘러싼 허다한 증인들이 있으니
모든 무거운 것과 얽매이기 쉬운 죄를 벗어 버리고
인내로써 우리 앞에 당한 경주를 하며
믿음의 주요 또 온전하게 하시는 이인 예수를 바라보자.

히브리서 12장 1절은 11장에서 살펴보았던 믿음의 조상들을 상기시키면서 우리 역시 믿음으로 인내해야 한다고 이야기합니다. 인생은 마라톤 경기와 같습니다. 우리는 구경꾼이 아니라 경기에 출전한 선수입니다. 어려운 환경에 굴복하거나 죄의 유혹에 빠지지 않고 오직 그리스도를 바라보며 믿음의 경주를 마쳤을 때 우리는 하나님이 예비하신 상을 받을 수 있습니다.

210
211

✎ 하루 한 문장, 생각 쓰기

오늘 본문을 쓰면서 깨달은 지혜, 새롭게 다짐한 점,
떠오른 생각 등을 자유롭게 적어 보세요.

Hebrews 13

Sacrifices Pleasing to God

1 Let brotherly love continue.

2 Do not neglect to show hospitality to strangers, for thereby some have entertained angels unawares.

3 Remember those who are in prison, as though in prison with them, and those who are mistreated, since you also are in the body.

4 Let marriage be held in honor among all, and let the marriage bed be undefiled, for God will judge the sexually immoral and adulterous.

5 Keep your life free from love of money, and be content with what you have, for he has said, "I will never leave you nor forsake you."

6 So we can confidently say, "The Lord is my helper; I will not fear; what can man do to me?"

7 Remember your leaders, those who spoke to you the word of God. Consider the outcome of their way of life, and imitate their faith.

8 Jesus Christ is the same yesterday and today and forever.

9 Do not be led away by diverse and strange teachings, for it is good for the heart to be strengthened by grace, not by foods, which have not benefited those devoted to them.

10　We have an altar from which those who serve the tent have no right to eat.

11　For the bodies of those animals whose blood is brought into the holy places by the high priest as a sacrifice for sin are burned outside the camp.

12　So Jesus also suffered outside the gate in order to sanctify* the people through his own blood.

13　Therefore let us go to him outside the camp and bear the reproach he endured.

14　For here we have no lasting city, but we seek the city that is to come.

15　Through him then let us continually offer up a sacrifice of praise to God, that is, the fruit of lips that acknowledge his name.

16　Do not neglect to do good and to share what you have, for such sacrifices are pleasing to God.

17　Obey your leaders and submit to them, for they are keeping watch over your souls, as those who will have to give an account. Let them do this with joy and not with groaning, for that would be of no advantage to you.

18　Pray for us, for we are sure that we have a clear conscience, desiring to act honorably** in all things.

19　I urge you the more earnestly to do this in order that I may be restored to you the sooner.

---

* 　sanctify [sǽŋktəfài] ⑧ ~을 신성하게 하다. 정화하다.
** 　honorably [ɑ́nərəbli] ⑲ 멋지게. 훌륭하게.

Benediction

20 Now may the God of peace who brought again from the dead our
Lord Jesus, the great shepherd of the sheep, by the blood of
the eternal covenant,

21 equip you with everything good that you may do his will, working
in us that which is pleasing in his sight, through Jesus Christ,
to whom be glory forever and ever. Amen.

Final Greetings

22 I appeal to you, brothers, bear with my word of exhortation,
for I have written to you briefly.

23 You should know that our brother Timothy has been released,
with whom I shall see you if he comes soon.

24 Greet all your leaders and all the saints. Those who come from
Italy send you greetings.

25 Grace be with all of you.

암송 구절 해설

Through him then let us continually offer up a sacrifice of praise to God,
that is, the fruit of lips that acknowledge his name. (13:15)

그러므로 우리는 예수로 말미암아 항상 찬송의 제사를 하나님께 드리자
이는 그 이름을 증언하는 입술의 열매니라.

15절은 진정한 예배가 무엇인지 이야기합니다. 그리스도인은 '예수로 말미암아' 항상
하나님께 찬송의 제사를 드립니다. 이는 호세아 선지자가 이야기한 것처럼 하나님의
이름을 증언하는 '입술의 열매'입니다. 하나님은 이처럼 하나님의 이름을 인정하며 찬
송하는 예배를 기뻐 받으십니다.

✏️ 하루 한 문장, 생각 쓰기

오늘 본문을 쓰면서 깨달은 지혜, 새롭게 다짐한 점,
떠오른 생각 등을 자유롭게 적어 보세요.

사랑을 더하면 온전해집니다.

이 모든 것 위에 사랑을 더하라 이는 온전하게 매는 띠니라(골 3:14).

도서출판 사랑플러스는 이 땅의 모든 교회와 성도들을 섬기기 위해 국제제자훈련원이 설립한 출판 사역 기관입니다.

십대를 위한 로마서·히브리서 영어로 한 달 쓰기

초판 1쇄 인쇄 2020년 11월 4일
초판 1쇄 발행 2020년 11월 11일

엮은이 사랑플러스 편집부

펴낸이 오정현
펴낸곳 사랑플러스
등록번호 제2002-000032호(2002년 2월 15일)
주소 서울시 서초구 효령로 68길 98(서초동)
전화 02)3489-4300   **팩스** 02)3489-4329
이메일 dmipress@sarang.org

ISBN 979-11-88402-08-3 43230

※ 책값은 뒤표지에 있습니다. 잘못된 책은 구입하신 곳에서 교환해드립니다.

로마서·히브리서 쓰기를 마치며 ✐

29일간 로마서 · 히브리서를 쓰면서 깨달은 점 등을 기록해 보세요.

	마친 날
	년. 월. 일.